Mental Toughness Training for Golf

by David Graham

with Guy Yocom

The Stephen Greene Press/Pelham Books

THE STEPHEN GREENE PRESS/PELHAM BOOKS

Published by the Penguin Group
Viking Penguin, a division of Penguin Books USA Inc., 375 Hudson
   Street, New York, New York, 10014, U.S.A.
Penguin Books Ltd., 27 Wrights Lane, London W8 5TZ, England
Penguin Books Australia Ltd., Ringwood, Victoria, Australia
Penguin Books Canada Ltd., 2801 John Street, Markham, Ontario,
   Canada L3R 1B4
Penguin Books (N.Z.) Ltd., 182-190 Wairau Road, Auckland 10,
   New Zealand

Penguin Books Ltd., Registered Offices: Harmondsworth, Middlesex,
England

First published in 1990 by The Stephen Greene Press/Pelham Books

Distributed by Viking Penguin, a division of Penguin Books USA Inc.

Photograph credits:
AP/Wide World Photos: Pages xii, xix, 3, 9, 11, 45, 50, 51, 55, 67, 68, 70,
78, 85, 88, 90, 94, 96, 98, 101, 104, 105, 108, 117, 121, 127, 130, 135, 137,
140, 142, 143, 147, 148, 153, 155
Yours in Sport (Lawrence Levy): Pages xiv, xv, xvii, 20, 24, 27, 30, 31,
34, 36, 38, 41, 47, 53, 57, 59, 64, 75, 81, 110, 115

Library of Congress Cataloging-in-Publication Data
Graham, David
    Mental toughness training for golf / by David Graham.
        p.   cm.
    ISBN 0-8289-0742-0
    1. Golf—Psychological aspects.   I. Title.
GV979.P75G73   1990
796.352′019—dc20   89-28815
                                                             CIP

Printed in the United States of America
Set in Galliard and Times Roman by Compset, Inc.
Designed by Ken Wilson
Produced by Unicorn Production Services, Inc.

Contents

Author's Note

This book was written in America, my home base for many years. Australian readers will notice that I use the U.S. system of measurement for distance, weights, etc. For those who have grown up with the metric system, a quick conversion table is provided below.

Minor changes have been made in the text where a turn of phrase was particularly "American," but the language of golf, like the game, is universal!

Conversions

U.S.	Metric
1 acre	0.405 hectares
1 foot	0.305 metres
1 yard	0.914 metres
1 mile	1.61 kilometres
1 pound	0.454 kilograms
1 ounce	28.3 grams
1 gallon	4.55 litres

Foreword

One important criterion for determining the level of mental toughness required for success in a fine motor skill sport such as golf is to measure the amount of downtime between shots. The more continuous the activity, the less demanding the sport typically is psychologically. Tennis, for example, is considered to be very challenging mentally because as much as 70 percent of the total match time is spent doing something other than playing points. Players wait to serve, return serve, change sides, and so forth. An average point lasts only seven to ten seconds followed by twenty to thirty seconds of rest. So much downtime and the stop-and-go nature of the sport mean lots of idle time to get yourself into trouble mentally—to lose concentration and focus. The continuous nature of sports like racquetball or handball makes them less challenging mentally.

And how about golf? Using the downtime measure, golf is clearly number one in difficulty. Less than 1 percent of your time on the course are you actually hitting balls. Ninety-nine percent plus is spent getting to the next ball, waiting, and setting up. That means you've got to control your mental activity 99 percent of the time. The activity demands of the sport simply do not automatically keep you focused and tuned in. And golf does not allow you to work out problems with nerves or frustrations physically—no jumping, sprinting, or jogging to work out the tension. Precise mental discipline and control 99 percent of the time—that's an impressive challenge to say the least. Because of this, the game of golf requires supreme mental toughness. All real greats in golf—Palmer, Nicklaus, Hogan, Norman, Player, Lopez, and Trevino—have displayed the mental discipline and

precision of Zen masters. Obviously their mental toughness was part of their genius.

The real question, however, is how did this part of their game come to be? Was their mental toughness a genetic gift? Were they simply born into the world mentally stronger than the rest? The research world of sports psychology answers that question with an emphatic no. From everything we know, mental toughness is an acquired skill that is understandable and operates according to the same laws of learning that apply to the physical world.

The simple fact is if you're not mentally tough you simply haven't learned the mental skills that make that happen. As a golfer you clearly understand the importance of mastering the fundamentals mechanically. Balance, rotation, follow-through, acceleration, grips, etc., have to be there for performance consistency to occur. And the same is true in the mental area. Relaxation, visualization, concentration, arousal control, and motivation represent psychological fundamentals in precisely the same sense.

David Graham has done a masterful job of translating generic material into a golf-specific mental toughness training program. His depth of knowledge of golf, his vast competitive experience, and his sensitivity and understanding for the mental arena are apparent. He makes the material come alive with realness and power through his rich world of personal experience and knowledge.

I am very excited about the job David has done with this book. I am also certain you will find David's work to be immensely helpful to your game. The greatest challenge of golf is clearly mental. David Graham has artfully crafted the plan that will enable you to win that ultimate challenge—the challenge of you against yourself.

Jim Loehr

Acknowledgments

All worthwhile things are not achieved without struggle, and this book is no exception. Thankfully, I had help from several talented people who poured heart and soul into the project.

First and foremost, I would like to thank Mr. James Loehr, Director of the Peak Performance Training Institute at Sonesta Santabel Harbour Resort. Jim, who also is Director of Sports Psychology at the Bollettieri Tennis Academy, is author of the book, *Mental Toughness Training for Sports,* a landmark work that has sharpened our insight into the application of sports psychology.

It is that work on which the basic outline of this book is based. Were it not for Jim's coherent perception of the elements of sports psychology, I could not have prepared this book in such an organized fashion. I am forever in his debt.

I would like to thank Guy Yocom of *Golf Digest* magazine. Without Guy's keen editing, sound foresight, and tireless work, this book would not have progressed through the many difficult stages of the editing process.

I also would like to thank the International Management Group, which has done a terrific job representing me in recent years. It was they who thought I would have something to offer other golfers in the area of sports psychology.

Thanks also to Gary Panks of Phoenix, Arizona. As my partner in the golf course design firm of Graham-Panks International, Gary has helped me start a whole new chapter in my life.

Finally, I would like to thank my wife, Maureen, for standing by me so unfailingly early in my career, when it often seemed I would never make it as a professional golfer. We now are in our

twenty-first year together, and she, along with my sons Andrew and Michael, has made me the happiest fellow on earth.

David Graham
Dallas, Texas
April 1989

Introduction
The New Age in Golf

In many ways, golf today is not the same game I saw and played ten years ago. New inroads into the areas of physical conditioning, golf equipment, nutrition, swing mechanics, and sports psychology have improved both our mental approach to the game and our physical ability to play it better. This is evident at all levels of the game. On the PGA Tour, Robert Wrenn shot a seventy-two-hole score of *27 under par* in winning the 1987 Buick Open. In his last year as an amateur, Billy Mayfair shot an opening-round 64 at Bear Creek in Denver, an incredibly difficult course, and went on to win the Pacific Coast Amateur by *fifteen strokes*. Scores in the low 60s are becoming commonplace. Players hit the ball farther than ever. They chip and putt better. They *think* better.

Much of this improvement can be attributed to simple evolution. Our knowledge and understanding of the mechanics of the golf swing have gradually increased, just as our knowledge has increased in fields such as medicine and biology. Today's golfers are for the most part bigger and stronger than their predecessors. There are more golfers playing the game and more golf courses on which to play. Some degree of improvement is going to occur over time due to the mere fact that golfers are maintaining interest in the game.

Another part of this evolution has to do with the tremendous amount of money available in professional golf today. Young golfers work very hard to one day have a chance at winning some of it. In 1989, PGA Tour purses exceeded $41 million, an all-time high. The Senior PGA Tour offered $10.5 million. The LPGA Tour is thriving, too. With that kind of money at stake,

Sandy Lyle typifies the modern tour pro: bigger, stronger, and more fit than his predecessors.

golf has become a big business, and players are constantly searching for an edge that will help them play better.

The other advances in golf must be credited to *revolution,* a forced awareness of factors that were previously unknown or ignored but that are gaining wider understanding and acceptance today. Elements of the game that would have been scoffed at ten or fifteen years ago are being appreciated for having very real value. In this regard, golf at the highest level is as much a science as it is an art form.

Physical fitness, for example, was once thought to be largely unnecessary for a golfer. On the PGA Tour today we have the Centinela Fitness Center, a traveling trailer that receives heavy use by the players. In it you can get a massage, sit in the whirlpool, or receive an ultrasound treatment for aching muscles. A trainer will bandage muscle pulls or sprains. They have high-protein fluids, heating creams, and medicine that relieves muscle soreness without making you drowsy. You can lift weights on state-of-the-art equipment, ride bicycle machines, or walk a treadmill. You can get a complete exercise program and advice on your diet.

Nutrition is receiving more attention. Gone are the days when players carried candy bars in their bags. Today they pack granola bars, apples, oranges, bananas, raisins, trail mix, and assorted nuts. Some players have personal nutritionists. A few, believe it or not, even carry bottled water with them. Most players prefer lean, nonfattening foods at dinnertime. You don't see many players hanging around bars at night, and few of the younger ones smoke cigarettes. They stay close to their hotel rooms, watch what they eat, and go to bed early.

Equipment is far superior to what it once was. Thirty years ago, shafts were inconsistent. So were the lofts and lies on most irons. A professional often had to tinker with a new set of clubs for six months before he got them just how he liked them. Those problems are almost nonexistent today. New clubshaft materials such as titanium and graphite have made it possible to hit the ball much farther. Golf balls are more consistent. Clubhead designs are much more advanced. Pros aren't the only ones who

Karsten Solheim, whose engineering research led to breakthroughs in club design that have helped golfers perform better.

David Leadbetter (right), *one of the keenest instructors in golf today, with one of his star pupils, Ove Sellberg of Sweden. Leadbetter is one of many teachers who display a profound knowledge of the golf swing.*

benefit; amateurs enjoy excellent quality control in the equipment they buy from golf shops and discount houses.

Advances in golf instruction have been considerable. Self-taught professionals like myself are rare. There are more good instructors, many of whom are brilliant and uncanny in their ability to detect minor swing flaws. A tour player who is struggling with his swing won't hesitate to pay $3,000 to have his personal instructor flown into a tournament site for a quick lesson. If that lesson sparks a $125,000 victory, it was well worth it. Instructors and their students today have at their disposal video cameras that quickly and accurately reveal details of the swing. There are even laboratories where players can go to study their biomechanical movements.

Junior golf has never been more organized or widespread. Children today learn the mechanics of the golf swing at an early age and increase their knowledge as they grow. The American

Junior Golf Association conducts a series of tournaments involving hundreds of youngsters. It resembles a tour, and by the time the children reach college, they are hardened competitors. College golf has also shown tremendous growth and provides a superb training ground for aspiring professionals. Almost all tour players fine-tuned their competitive skills in college.

But for all of these advances, the biggest inroads have been made in the area of sports psychology. That's what this book is about. Twenty years ago, any formal study of the mental side of golf would have been considered far-out and impractical. I recall an instance in the 1960s when Bert Yancey followed Jack Nicklaus with a stopwatch to monitor how long Jack took with his preshot routine. In a tournament that Nicklaus won, Yancey found that Jack never varied his routine by more than three seconds. A few pros were impressed, but surprisingly, many others just shrugged it off.

Today there is solid evidence that sports psychology has a useful place in golf. An impressive example of this occurred at the 1988 Dunhill Cup at St. Andrews in Scotland. The Australian team, represented by Rodger Davis, Greg Norman, and me, was playing very well and had a chance to win on the last day. Rodger was playing steady golf and had a one-stroke lead over Ireland's Des Smyth as he came to the tee of the par-4 seventeenth, the infamous Road Hole where many dreams have been shattered. Rodger hit his tee shot out-of-bounds, took a triple bogey 7 on the hole, and lost. He was absolutely devastated. On the plane to London that night, he was inconsolable. Tears came to his eyes. "I've failed," he said. "I'm sorry, I let everyone down, it was my fault." He was extremely hard on himself.

Setbacks like this sometimes destroy careers. Ed Sneed was never quite the same after he bogeyed the last three holes at the 1979 Masters and ultimately lost to Fuzzy Zoeller in a play-off. Tony Jacklin will admit that losing the 1972 British Open to Lee Trevino took something out of him he has been unable to recover. For Rodger Davis, a similar outcome was possible. But Rodger took action. He saw a sports psychologist who promised help with his game. "Your problem is simple," the sports psy-

Rodger Davis, who overcame a devastating blow to his self-confidence with the help of a sports psychologist.

chologist said. "You're not concentrating on your routine. Get that squared away and you'll be fine."

Rodger did as he was told. He concentrated on nothing except his preshot routine. There was no room in his mind for negative thinking, self-doubt, or memories of the Dunhill Cup. With his swing rhythm fully restored, Rodger went home and won the Australian Bi-Centennial Golf Classic and the $500,000 prize that went with it. He was a new man, totally reborn, all because of the psychological help he received.

Examples like this offer irrefutable proof that the relationship between mind and body is critical. In golf, the ability to execute physically what our mind tells us is the factor that separates good players from great ones. The world is filled with incredibly talented players who had superb physical skills but were somehow held back by an inability to control their thoughts and emotions. On the other hand, there are some golfers, such as Calvin Peete, whose strong mental skills have compensated for physical shortcomings, in Calvin's case a permanently bent left arm.

Sports psychologists are quite visible on the PGA Tour today. Dr. Bob Rotella, Dr. Don Greene, Dr. Richard Coop, and others have had impressive results in improving the mental approach of many players. They are unlocking the doors to the mind and tapping its vast potential. Nevertheless, there is still a long way to go. Although we know that the process of playing well may be as much as 90 percent mental, we are still searching for the knowledge and understanding that will help us formulate a surefire teaching methodology that will work for everyone. Still, we are making progress, and it is my belief that by studying the techniques presented in this book you can improve your performance substantially.

The challenge to improve your mental toughness is formidable, for golf is unique. In many other sports, sheer determination and hard work will pay dividends. In golf, that is not always true. It is an elusive, bewitching game that requires a more intelligent approach. It takes knowledge, some physical effort, and the right mental attitude. Finding the proper blend of

Calvin Peete, who has a permanently bent left arm due to a boyhood accident, overcame his infirmity with self-discipline, perseverance, and a strong will to succeed.

these ingredients and applying them correctly is a tremendous challenge that few golfers respond to effectively. However, when those elements come together, as they do for everyone on occasion, the sensation is magical. Those occasions are what make golf the addictive game that it is.

As we will discuss in chapter 3, there is a constellation of mental skills that, when applied correctly, will allow you to realize your full potential as a golfer. At the PGA Tour level, a weakness in only one or two of these key psychological areas is enough to prevent a player from earning or keeping his playing privileges. The tour is that competitive. You, the amateur, have more latitude. Improving your proficiency in most areas will dramatically improve your game, heighten your enjoyment, and give you more self-satisfaction than you thought possible.

The sum of these mental skills is mental toughness. When you become resilient to adversity, learn to control your emotions, and make your body perform the way your mind tells it, you have mental toughness. Jack Nicklaus has it. Seve Ballesteros has it. Chances are, your club champion has it.

Whatever your aspirations are in golf, they have to be earned. Golf is a game you play against *yourself.* There is no one to blame for your failures except you. The credit for your successes goes to you alone. It is a game that demands self-reliance, discipline, and responsibility for your actions. The more you put into it, the more you get out of it.

You have a tremendous advantage over golfers of the past. You have the benefit of their knowledge and experience, imparted to you through instruction books and magazines. You have ready access to qualified instructors. You have a head start in undertaking the pleasurable search for improvement from which you will derive deep satisfaction.

Most of all, you have the opportunity, through this book and others like it, to gain a deeper understanding of *yourself* and the ways your mind influences your physical actions. I am convinced that this is the key to the new frontier in golf, and I take great pleasure in joining you in this quest.

David Graham's Playing Record

1967   Queensland PGA, Australia

1970   Tasmanian Open
Victorian Open, Australia
Thailand Open
Yomiuri Classic, Japan
French Open
World Cup (with Bruce Devlin)

1971   Caracas Open, Venezuela
JAL Open, Japan

1972   Cleveland Open

1975   Wills Masters, Australia

1976   Chunichi Crowns, Japan
Westchester Classic
American Golf Classic
Piccadilly World Match Play, England

1977   Australian Open

1978   Mexican Cup

1979   PGA Championship
West Lakes Classic, Australia
Air New Zealand Open

1980   Memorial Tournament
Heublin Classic, Brazil
Rolex World Mixed Team Championship (with Jan
Stephenson)
Mexican Open

1981   Phoenix Open
U.S. Open
Lancome Trophy, France

1982   Lancome Trophy, France

1983   Houston Open

1985   Queensland Open, Australia
        Dunhill Cup (with Greg Norman, Graham Marsh)

1986   Dunhill Cup (with Greg Norman, Rodger Davis)

        Career earnings on PGA Tour through 1988:
        $1,815,780.
        Total career earnings, worldwide: $4,000,000.

1

Learning from My Personal Struggle

Looking back, it awes me to think how much easier my career in golf would have been had I known how to achieve mental toughness at a younger age. Success tends to erase much of the pain, frustration, discouragement, and torment of my early years; but suffice to say, much of it was pure hell. This was due in part to mechanical deficiencies in my golf swing, but a great deal of it was the result of an extremely poor mental attitude and my inability to control my emotions on the course.

Many of my mental problems in golf can be traced to struggles in my personal life, as I'll explain later. Most of them, however, can be attributed to my not knowing how to approach the game with the right frame of mind. Like many amateurs, I knew my attitude was bad but didn't know how to go about improving it. I had a fierce temper and very little patience. I lacked composure. I was a painfully slow player, so much so that other professionals dreaded being paired with me. I was a brooder and a loner who kept to himself as much as possible. I was perpetually angry with myself and others for reasons that now seem ridiculous. In sum, I was deeply insecure and scared to death of showing emotion to anyone. This did not bode well for my game.

Somehow, I succeeded in spite of myself. My anger, frustration, and sheer desperation served to make me incredibly determined. I practiced harder than anyone, studied the game diligently, and was utterly single-minded in my purpose to become a good player. After about ten years this approach began to pay off. But what a price I paid!

Once I attained some material success by winning several big tournaments, my personal life and demeanor on the golf course began to stabilize. My attitude gradually improved, and that is when I became aware of the importance of a sound mental approach. What's more, I learned how to achieve it. Soon after I gained this new understanding, I finally came of age as a golfer and person. Not only did I break through and win the 1979 PGA Championship, 1981 U.S. Open, and many other titles, I began to enjoy the game and my life more. I made new friends. I became a better husband and father. I became a better human being.

It is unnecessary for you to take the same route I did. Had I known all I know now about managing myself as well as my golf game, I'm convinced I would have tasted success much earlier, at a much lower price. With the vast knowledge and information available to golfers today, there is no reason for you not to improve your game. And take it from me, most of this great game is mental.

It is my hope that, through understanding my personal struggles and subsequent achievements, I can help you learn to improve your game and enjoy it more. I believe that all golfers, regardless of ability, are subject to the same set of psychological problems. At some time we all have trouble coping with pressure, accepting bad breaks, fighting the golf swing, staying motivated, controlling our emotions, and trying to stay relaxed. I will outline the causes and cures for problems such as these in this book.

I sincerely think that golf is the best game man has devised. It is the most rewarding, the most challenging, and the most fun. Regardless of the level you play at, it is sure to give you a terrific return on your investment of time and effort.

The Early Years: Trial, Tribulation, and Very Little Success

It isn't necessary for me to divulge every detail of my life story, but I think that by offering a glimpse into some of my experiences, you may be able to relate to some of my emotions

Words can't describe the joy I felt when I won the 1981 U.S. Open Championship at Merion Golf Club in Ardmore, Pennsylvania. It signaled the end of my long and torturous battle with myself.

and even see a part of yourself in me. My attitudes toward success and failure were extremely counterproductive and are, I think, common among golfers of all abilities.

The setting of my life and the circumstances that spawned my long personal battle with myself were unique. I grew up in Melbourne, Australia, with my mother, father, and older sister. Our financial situation could best be described as lower middle class. Ours was not a happy home. My father and mother fought often and I can still recall their arguing. This led, I think, to some of my insecurity later on.

I started playing golf at age twelve at Wattle Park, a small nine-hole course in Melbourne. I got my first set of clubs out of our garage. They belonged to my mother, Patricia, and they were left-handed. So, even though I was a natural right-hander, I began knocking the ball around southpaw fashion and within a year had acquired a legitimate 1-handicap. That may imply that I had a lot of raw talent, but in fact I did little else in my spare time except hit balls. I had few friends and got into a lot of fights, none of which I won due to my small size. I was an average-to-poor student and often would skip school and ride my bike to Wattle Park to practice. My first triumph was the Wattle Park Junior Championship, and I was awarded a tiny little trophy that I still have.

My love for golf was exceeded only by my hatred of school, and at age fourteen I told my mother I wanted to quit and become a professional golfer. Knowing where my heart was, she gave in. My father, however, would have none of it. He was a stern man who didn't take kindly to being defied, and he told me that if I quit school, he would kick me out of the house. I quit school and, domestically, all hell broke loose. I was allowed to stay in the house, although I was quartered in the back part of it with my mother. My father and older sister lived in the front part of the house, and I hardly ever saw them.

I took a job at Riversdale Golf Club where the pro, an extremely kind man named George Naismith, took me under his wing. There I worked like a slave, taking only one day off every two weeks. I often worked twelve hours a day, doing every odd

job you can think of. My salary was eight pounds (about fifteen dollars) a week. I channeled every free moment I had into practicing. Between the ages of fifteen and seventeen, when I wasn't working around the club, I was on the practice range hitting balls. I would hit them and pick them up, hit them and pick them up, until it was too dark to see. Sometimes I would sleep on the sofa in the pro shop instead of going home.

Because my home environment wasn't very happy, Riversdale became my refuge. It was a nice club. I had to wear a collar and tie and be on my best behavior at all times. I was young and, socially, quite green. On occasion I would call a member by his wrong name and get in trouble for it, but Mr. Naismith was always there to bail me out. There is no question that if it weren't for his help, I would have become a juvenile delinquent. I had no friends my own age and, hence, none of the companionship that is so important to young teenagers.

I became an assistant professional when I was seventeen. Mr. Naismith had never given me help with my swing, but one day he came over to where I was practicing and watched me hit balls. Although I was a scratch player left-handed, he insisted that I play right-handed. Competitively, I had played in several assistant pro tournaments left-handed and had even had a little success. But after the change, I went into total obscurity for about eighteen months. I finally won a tournament playing right-handed. I can still break 80 playing left-handed, although I never was as good as, say, Mac O'Grady, who is a phenomenal ball striker from either side.

One day Mr. Naismith resigned from Riversdale, which left me with nowhere to go. Sensing this, he arranged for me to take the professional's job at a nine-hole course in Tasmania, the island state south of the Australian mainland. It didn't take long for me to go stone broke there. I knew nothing about retailing and ordered too much equipment. I was persuaded to purchase a car that I couldn't afford. Things were extremely difficult at this point in my life. I sank about $6,000 into debt and became utterly depressed. I thought the world was against me. Then one day a fellow professional named Eric Cremin came to the club

to do a promotion for a Sydney-based equipment company, Precision Golf Forgings. He took me aside. "Son, you're a pretty good player," he said. "You've got to get out of this place. You're digging a hole for yourself here that you might never get out of. It's a waste of time. Come with me to Sydney and I'll get you a job with our golf company."

I knew he was right. I sold the equipment in the shop, packed my bags, and moved to Sydney, where I lived in a boarding house. I had just turned eighteen. My work at PGF consisted mainly of doing errands, but I also learned how to balance and swing-weight clubs and custom-fit them for people.

As for playing, my tournament competition was limited to Monday pro-ams. Soon after, however, I went on what was known as the Queensland Tour, and that's where my life hit rock bottom. It's painful to look back on those days. I was still in debt from my job in Tasmania, my game was awful, and emotionally I was a miserable wreck. I had less natural ability than anyone on the circuit and was reminded of this often by players and outsiders. My self-esteem was very low. While other players received such perks as lessons, free clubs, and balls, I couldn't even find a place to practice. I wound up spending 90 percent of my time practicing on a shabby football field, where I was kicked off regularly for hitting the balls too far over the field onto a road.

I managed a few nice finishes on the Queensland circuit, but realistically I had little chance of succeeding as a professional golfer. Nobody was willing to help me and I didn't know how to help myself. The depth of my despair is difficult for most people to comprehend, especially people who have never been in my situation. I came close to quitting a hundred times. I was forever being told things like, "You're too small." "You're not strong enough." "You have no talent." "Your swing is no good." "Find something else to do." It was one thing not to have any encouragement but quite another to have to endure constant criticism from people who wouldn't think of offering any help.

All of the put-downs and negative comments made me respond in one way: more physical effort. Somehow I sensed that

if I worked harder than anybody else, I would eventually be rewarded for it. I became an utter workaholic at golf. I worked on my game every day, all day long. Nobody can stand on a practice range from sunup to sundown, of course, but a typical day would start with me chipping and putting when the sun came up, followed by eighteen holes. I'd eat some fish and chips for lunch, play eighteen more holes, then hit balls until I was exhausted. Then I would go chip and putt some more. I'd drag myself home, fall into bed, get up the next day, and do it all over again.

Golf was all I knew and that knowledge was a source of motivation. Fortunately I liked it, but I was plainly aware that because of my lack of education, if I failed at golf I would be in serious trouble. I was feeling even more desperate. Pro-am tournaments in those days had a total purse of $500. First place was worth $100, and I needed that money in the worst possible way. I began to consider every single shot in every tournament as a life-or-death proposition, which, in a way, it was. I was chronically slow. I had a violent temper, throwing clubs all the time and arguing with every person in sight. Socially I came off as cocky and arrogant, which in retrospect was simply a cry for attention. "Hey, I'm alive," I was saying. "Somebody help me." I needed help with my game, with my finances, with my mental attitude. But at this point, nobody wanted to listen.

Mechanically, my game was lousy. My swing was almost entirely self-taught. It was flat, wristy, and produced a low, ugly hook. It didn't hold up very well under pressure. I got the ball into the hole by sheer force of will. Physically, I was terribly intimidated by other players. I weighed 132 pounds and had a twenty-eight-inch waist. I gradually built myself up by exercising religiously. One time I damn near killed myself when I accidentally dropped a set of barbells on my head.

Still haunted by debts, my mental game became worse. Because of my slow play, poor manners, and tendency to complain to everyone, I was disliked by most of the other players. And I hated myself. I had more feelings of failure than I can express. For years these feelings manifested in strange ways. When I later played the Asian Tour, for instance, I used to fake being

sick if I had a bad round. I was always making excuses. This is hard for me to admit now. If I made a friend, I'd lose him right away by starting some silly argument. I refused to socialize with people. Instead of going to the beach or to parties, I virtually lived at the golf course and in my hotel. I had no sense of caring for others, no sense of humor, no zest for living.

I didn't know it at the time, but my stint on the Queensland Tour resulted in the single most important blessing in my life. I met my wife, the former Maureen Burdett, at the Cairns Open. We dated briefly, but I didn't see her again until the tour returned to Cairns a year later.

I was loyal to no one and, not surprisingly, no one was loyal to me. This changed when I came back to Cairns the following year and married Maureen. At last, I had found someone I could trust and someone I felt cared for me. Maureen's presence seemed to remove some of the immense pressure I placed on myself. Then I made two more lasting friends in Norman Von Nida and Alex Mercer, both of whom were terrific players. I remember Mercer taking me fishing a couple of times and telling me, "David, you've got to get away like this more often. You can't eat, sleep, and drink golf. You've got to take a break." I distinctly recall my answer to him: "Why?" I really didn't understand what he was getting at. In fact, I refused to go fishing with him until after 8:00 P.M., when it was too dark to practice.

But with Maureen behind me, my attitude gradually began to come around. Some of my feelings of desperation disappeared and so did many of the negative aspects of my personality. My approach to the game became a little more relaxed, and when that happened I really started having some success. In 1969, at age twenty-three, Precision Golf Forgings selected me to represent them on the Asian Tour. Their sponsorship was limited to paying my airfare, and I stayed in people's houses all over the circuit. I played in the Philippines, Malaysia, Singapore, India, Hong Kong, Thailand, Korea, Taiwan, and Japan. I did fairly well. I finished second in the Singapore Open and won $2,800. I still remember how that money seemed like an absolute fortune. A couple of weeks later, I won the Thailand Open and another

An early breakthrough: winning the Yomiuri Invitational in April 1970. The $7,500 check eased my inner feeling of desperation, but my mental attitude still needed improvement.

healthy check. I then went to Japan and won the Yomiuri Invitational, banking $7,500 and winning a new car.

Despite the slight improvement in my self-perception and outlook on life, my behavior on the Asian Tour was in many ways abominable and reflected my inner torment. I was still my own worst enemy, on and off the golf course. I used to scream at the bus driver for wanting to shuttle the players back to the hotel at 4:00 P.M. when, as I saw it, there was plenty of daylight left to practice. I continued to work like the devil. I was always the last one to leave the practice range, and to my way of thinking, there wasn't enough time in the day for me to get the practice I needed.

I felt that the only way to earn respect and attention was to play and practice harder. At this point I could afford, as a result of my winnings, to have Maureen join me in Asia. One day she

asked me, "David, why do you act so badly on the golf course when you're a totally different person off it? Why do people dislike you when I think you're a very nice person?" My feeble answer was, "It helps me play better." But I knew it wasn't true and I resolved to change my attitude.

Turnaround and Breakthrough

The next year, 1970, I won a $10,000 bonus for being the leading player on the Asian circuit. Brimming with overconfidence, I came to America and tried to qualify for the PGA Tour. I failed. That was a setback, but a couple of weeks later a very positive thing happened. I was selected, through an odd set of circumstances, to represent Australia at the 1970 World Cup in Buenos Aires, Argentina. My partner was Bruce Devlin. We won the tournament and I finished second individually. I flew down to Argentina in coach class and flew back in first class. Not only was this my first taste of big-league competition, it was my first close exposure to a world-class golfer. Devlin was everything I was not: a tremendous player, a well-liked person, and someone who handled everything with incredible grace and composure. I admired him immensely and wanted to be more like him.

I earned my PGA Tour card the following year. My finishing 135th on the money list showed that after eight years as a professional, working on my game virtually full time, neither my golf swing nor my mental attitude were good enough for me to compete against the best golfers in the world. The next year, however, I won the Cleveland Open and, with earnings of more than $57,000, finished 35th on the money list. The next two years offered more moderate success.

If I were to really break through, however, I knew I would have to improve my perception of myself and my golf game. Although a major swing change had transformed me into a pretty fair ball striker, mentally I was the same negative, desperate person. In 1974 I actively began working on my mental attitude. It was only when I began to make a little progress that I began to see how appalling my attitude was. For instance, Jack Nicklaus,

Winning the 1970 World Cup for Australia with Bruce Devlin (second from right) gave me my first taste of big-league competition. More important, Devlin set an example, personally and professionally, that I was to follow the rest of my career.

whom I had become friends with, had asked me for some advice on the design of MacGregor golf clubs. I agreed to attend a meeting of MacGregor executives. When a point about club design arose, I blurted to the president of the company, "You have no idea what you're talking about. Why the hell did you ask me up here if you don't want my opinion?" This was a mistake, of course. This type of blustery behavior was all a front, because privately I was very self-critical.

The search for more self-control was puzzling. There were no sports psychologists on the PGA Tour at that time, at least none that I knew about, and I was left to sort it out for myself. However, I began to read stories by the top players, about the techniques they used to feel comfortable and controlled on the course and how they were able to maintain their concentration and composure so they could play to their full potential. My friendship with Nicklaus gave me insight into his inner strength,

and he inspired me to copy some of his techniques and mannerisms. For instance, I noticed that Jack wore a stare when he played that was almost a scowl. "I'm going to get me one of those stares," I told Maureen. I began to make friends and socialize more, going to Christmas parties and other social functions. I began to play practice rounds with my new friends. I even began to have a glass of wine now and then. To that point in my life, I had never touched liquor.

Progress came in small steps. One thing that really helped was the birth of my oldest son, Andrew, in 1974. Suddenly my responsibilities extended beyond myself and my wife. I had always been incredibly selfish, but with Andrew in the world I had a whole new set of reasons for wanting to improve and play well. Instead of, "I'm going to do it because I need the money and to show all my critics that they were wrong about me," my motivations became different. I aspired to become a top professional because I *wanted* to, because it would provide security for my family as well as a great deal of self-satisfaction. It's ironic how an increase in responsibility actually resulted in me putting less pressure on myself.

As it turned out, my attitude changed my performance, when all along I thought it would take good performance to change my attitude. I used all kinds of little mental tricks to help me play better. Some of them worked, some didn't. For instance, I resolved to be more like Nicklaus in that I would never show emotion when I got a bad break, even if my insides felt like a kitchen blender. I wanted to look cool and began trying to do that regardless of how I felt inside. As a result, I started to *feel* cool as well. It helped. On the other hand, I once thought it would be helpful to be as relaxed as possible on the golf course. Unfortunately, I got so relaxed I played like a sleepwalker.

You live and learn. As my life became more ordered and my new mental attitude began to bear results, it made it easier for more successes to follow. I began to play golf instead of the game playing me. By the time I won the 1979 PGA Championship and 1981 U.S. Open, I had attained a certain control of my mental state and had a fine facility for dealing with the many ups and downs one faces during a round of golf.

I'm still learning, of course. I don't believe anyone will ever master the game, mentally or physically, but I do believe that even amateurs can learn to transcend the most common mental pitfalls involved in playing golf. There is no question that the skills required to do this are acquired, not inherited, because if anyone ever inherited a bad attitude, it was I.

There's a popular, funny saying that goes, "90 percent of the game is half mental." I couldn't agree more. Now let's get to work on mastering the mental side of this fascinating game.

2

Why Is Golf So Hard?
Inherent Problems, Practical Solutions

Golf is unquestionably the most difficult game in the world to play well. Every professional and low-handicap amateur will agree with me on this. I've played with athletes from many other sports and have never met one who didn't hold the professional golfer in complete awe. In all modesty, I can see their point. It took me many long years to become proficient at golf, yet I still make mental and physical mistakes every time I play. For the amateur who lacks my knowledge, training, and skill, learning to hit a ball with the authority and apparent ease of a tour pro truly seems incredible.

What makes golf so challenging, so maddeningly difficult? How can the game turn you inside out emotionally, making you feel euphoric one minute and completely frustrated the next? Why is it so easy on some days and impossible on others?

The answer, I feel, lies in the nature of the game. It is impossible to master. I've devoted almost my entire life to golf and yet am still prone to making physical and mental mistakes. So are my peers. Hale Irwin lost the 1983 British Open by one stroke after whiffing a six-inch putt in the third round. Jack Nicklaus shot an 83 in the British Open of 1981. Tommy Nakajima botched the 1984 British Open at St. Andrews when he took four shots to escape from a bunker on the seventeenth hole. Tom Weiskopf made a 13 on the par-3 twelfth hole at Augusta National in the 1980 Masters.

As I see it, amateurs would benefit by understanding how

difficult the game is. It is hard for them to accept bad shots, tough luck, slumps, and the slowness with which they improve. They get discouraged. They scold themselves. They take it out on family and friends. Sometimes they quit playing altogether. In sum, their lack of perspective prevents them from enjoying the things that led them to play golf in the first place.

The key is to recognize the inherent difficulty of the game and learn how to respond with enthusiasm and determination. Professionals have learned how to do this, and it is one of the things that separates them from the good amateur. Only when you can identify the different ways that golf works on you emotionally and psychologically can you move on to the more advanced techniques for acquiring mental toughness that we'll discuss later in this book.

Let's explore some of the characteristics of golf that make it so difficult. My guess is that you haven't thought of all of them before. Note my advice on how to approach each one rationally and productively.

Golf Is Time Consuming

The most subtle element working against the golfer is time. The game takes four and a half hours or longer to play, very little of which is devoted to actually hitting the ball. That leaves plenty of time to ponder poor shots, not-so-friendly playing partners, the slow group in front of you, or that night's activities at home. How you react to outside stimulation and how well you control your thoughts, attitudes, and emotions has a profound effect on how you play. Managing your downtime effectively during a round is an important part of the game and is something every professional does extremely well.

Here are some keys to handling problems related to the time element in golf.

Keep Your Emotions in Check

The first pitfall related to time is the tendency to experience extreme highs and lows. Golf has a way of sending you on an

emotional roller coaster. It's not uncommon to feel fear, frustration, exhilaration, anger, joy, and discouragement in the same round—or even on the same hole. This would be damaging enough if a round consisted of only nine holes, but over a long eighteen-hole round it is especially debilitating. The game becomes tedious and you deplete much-needed reserves of physical and mental energy.

Ideally, you should remain on an even keel emotionally regardless of what happens. No one is more adept at this than Greg Norman. In the 1984 U.S. Open at Winged Foot Golf Club in Mamaroneck, New York, Norman was locked in a very close duel with Fuzzy Zoeller as he played the back nine on Sunday. To that point in his career, Norman had shown great promise, and the media was putting tremendous pressure on him to break through and win a major championship. He now had that chance. If he won, it would galvanize his standing as one of the great players in the world. A great deal of money and fame would follow. If he lost, all kinds of negative labels would be applied to him, and there was no telling where his career would go from there.

Winged Foot is an extremely demanding golf course to begin with, but for the 1984 Open the U.S. Golf Association had narrowed the landing areas off the tees and let the thick bent-grass rough grow extremely high around the firm, fast, undulating greens. When Hale Irwin won the U.S. Open there in 1974, his winning total was 7 over par, one of the highest seventy-two-hole scores in relation to par in recent U.S. Open history. Norman was handling these conditions very well in the final round and was pumped up as he came to the par-4 sixteenth hole.

At 452 yards, the sixteenth plays as a par 5 for the members. Greg hit an extremely long, straight drive. He was definitely up emotionally then, facing only an iron shot to the green. Unfortunately, he pulled his second shot left of the green into that tall Open rough, where he faced an all but impossible up and down for par. When he saw his lie, he immediately felt down. Yet, somehow, he gouged the ball out with his sand wedge to within a foot or two of the pin. He made his par. He was up again. On

the 444-yard seventeenth, another backbreaking par 4, he pulled his drive into a clump of trees off of the fairway. He was down again, knowing full well that any mistake could cost him the greatest victory of his career. Norman punched his ball out onto the fairway and then, using all of his strength, hit an incredible recovery shot onto the green. From there, he made a terrific putt for his par. He was up again. How many emotional ups and downs has he experienced so far?

On the par-4 eighteenth, one of the great finishing holes in golf, Greg split the fairway with another terrific tee shot. In 1974, Hale Irwin needed a 2-iron to reach the green. Greg needed only a 6-iron. He proceeded to hit his worst shot of the day, blocking his approach into the grandstand twenty yards right of the green. He was down again, maybe permanently, because it is just about impossible to hit the ball close to the pin from there. Greg hit a superb recovery shot under the circumstances, just over the green in light fringe about forty feet from the hole. Still, he had to be feeling down.

What Norman did next tells you something about his incredible emotional stability. From a spot where taking two putts would have prompted a nice ovation from the crowd, Greg holed the putt. More important, he did everything possible to give himself a chance to make it. Instead of feeling dejected about "blowing" the U.S. Open, he pulled himself together. He had the composure, toughness, and awareness to read the green carefully, go through his preshot routine with precision, and make a beautiful stroke.

Greg wound up tied with Zoeller. The fact that Greg lost the eighteen-hole play-off the next day is incidental. The point is, Greg never felt as up after his great shots on the closing holes as you might think, nor did he feel as down after his bad shots as he probably had the right to feel. With the U.S. Open at stake, Greg had enough discipline and self-control to keep his emotions in check at every moment. Had he allowed himself to become exhilarated with the par he made on the sixteenth hole, his poor drive on the seventeenth would have been such an emotional blow that he probably wouldn't have had the composure to hit the brilliant recovery he did. Conversely, when he hit his bad

shot on the eighteenth, he didn't give himself time to feel let down. He immediately focused his attention on the next shot, which, when you think about it, is the only one that matters.

All of this isn't to say that you should behave like an impassive robot on the course. A good shot should give you a psychological lift. A bad shot should prompt you to kick yourself in the pants and inspire you to do better on the next one. Show me a golfer who is bankrupt emotionally and I'll show you a golfer who will never play to his full potential. My point is, you should make any shot, good or bad, work *for* you in some way.

In the forthcoming chapters, I'll explain in more detail how you can employ certain techniques to combat extremes of emotional highs and lows.

Maintain Your Inner Rhythm

Regardless of the sport, all athletes perform better when they utilize their inner clock, a form of internal rhythm that aids the process of thinking and hitting golf shots. It is a learned skill (as we'll discuss later) that you can eventually perform subconsciously. Other athletes have it. For instance, a basketball player dribbles the ball with a steady rhythm even though his conscious mind is focused on a play that is developing. A distance runner times his strides perfectly without conscious thought and is so good at it that he can tell you within a few seconds how fast he ran a mile. A football quarterback drops back to pass and sees a wall of linemen rushing in to tackle him, yet he remains unconsciously aware of how long it takes a chosen receiver to complete his route.

Golfers not only have this inner rhythm, they need it to play their best. Establishing and sustaining this rhythm is difficult because you are on the course for so long and because so many unexpected things can happen that disrupt your inner rhythmic flow. You are headed for trouble when this inner rhythm is broken. Sometimes you can even see it happen. Sam Snead loves to tell of his experience in the 1942 PGA Championship. Facing Jim Turnesa in the thirty-six-hole final, the match stood dead

even as Turnesa prepared to drive from the twenty-eighth tee. To that point in the match, Snead noted that Turnesa waggled the driver exactly two times before beginning the backswing. Now, with the pressure on, he watched Turnesa waggle *four* times. Right there, Sam knew he had Turnesa on the ropes. Sure enough, Turnesa hit his drive in the trees. Snead, buoyed with confidence, won the hole and eventually won the match on the thirty-fifth hole.

It doesn't take the pressure of a PGA Championship to throw your rhythm off. Sometimes the slightest thing can make you lose it. For instance, have you ever searched for a lost ball and felt anxious because you might be holding up the group behind you? Chances are you probably hit your next shot in haste. Or, have you ever hit a bunker shot and then scrambled to rake the sand so you can get to your ball in time to putt without delay? Chances are your first putt was not very good. Incidents like these bring on anxiety and destroy inner rhythm. Instead of playing these shots in a calm, relaxed manner using your normal swing tempo and rhythm, your inner clock is thrown out of sync. Your thought process changes, your preshot routine changes, and the pace of your swing changes as well.

My advice is to remain as placid as possible regardless of what odd things happen. You can't help losing a ball on occasion, so don't let yourself become frantic or upset just because you might hold someone up a couple of minutes. These things happen. You can always step up the pace a little on the next hole. You can learn to walk quickly between shots so that any time devoted to using the bathroom, looking for a lost ball, or going back to the last green to retrieve a forgotten putter is more easily absorbed into the course of the round. You can always be ready to hit when it's your turn. You can encourage your playing partners to keep moving. Just don't put yourself in position to upset your rhythm with a sudden change of pace in play.

A big part of establishing inner rhythm is learning a preshot routine. In virtually every sport, the critical motion is undertaken while the athlete is moving. The baseball pitcher has his windup. In basketball, the foul shooter dips his knees a little prior to releasing the ball. The tenpin bowler takes several

Performing my preshot routine. The process is critical, for it instills inner rhythm and programs you for the shot you are about to play.

strides before sending the ball down the lane. This motion sharpens timing, enhances rhythm, and loosens tension in the body.

Unfortunately, golfers do not have this luxury. The swing is undertaken from a static start. When you are settled in at address, you are motionless until you start the backswing. This is a tremendous detriment. With your body still and your mind focused on the ball, it is easy for physical tension and mental anxiety to set in. I call it the "freeze zone." Inner rhythm is destroyed and when you finally take the club back, your swing tempo is disrupted and your mental focus is unsteady.

Adopting a preshot routine and repeating it on every swing will help you establish inner rhythm. A preshot routine gives you a "running start" of sorts. When PGA Tour players practice, they usually aren't too preoccupied with their swing mechanics. That aspect of their game is sound already. Most of the time they are searching for the perfect internal rhythm that allows them to address the ball and pull the trigger without having to consciously think about it. When the pressure is on, it is a lack of rhythm, not poor swing mechanics, that presents the biggest problem.

Preshot routines vary, but here is one you might try to copy.

1. When you arrive at the ball, set the bag down in the same place every time. Position it, for example, five feet to the right of your ball and three feet down the target line. This makes the rest of your routine easier to follow.

2. Assess the shot. First, examine the lie. Next, calculate the correct yardage. Third, note the elevation of the green. Finally, determine the direction and force of the wind.

3. Choose the correct club. Remove it from the bag and sight the ball and the target from down the target line. Visualize the ball flying at the target with the optimum trajectory.

4. Approach the ball deliberately, keeping your eyes only on the ball and the target. Be precise about your alignment. Heft the club lightly in your hands to promote feel in your hands and arms.

5. After you seat the clubhead behind the ball, step in with your right foot, first, then with your left. Now make any final adjustments in your stance so you feel comfortable.

6. Look at the target and down at the ball three times. This is called "locking in" on the shot and is the final step before you start the backswing.

7. Take the club back and swing through in one smooth, continuous motion.

Developing your own preshot routine requires practice. You must go through the exact same steps every time and take the same amount of time on every shot. Never vary your routine. When you hit balls on the practice range, perform your preshot routine "by the numbers." Actually count the number of seconds you stand over the ball before taking the club back. Experiment until you find a time frame that is comfortable for you, as it will vary depending on your individual temperament. Once you find a time frame that is comfortable, repeat it over and over again until it becomes automatic. It should never, ever change. Once you ingrain this element into your game, you'll be surprised at how your ball striking improves.

There is one other way to establish this rhythm and set the swing in motion, and that's the waggle. It should be performed during step 6 of your routine. Ben Hogan talked about the waggle extensively in his book, *Five Lessons: The Modern Fundamentals of Golf.* He noted that the waggle not only provides rhythm but helps from a mechanical standpoint as well. Try it and see if it works. It may or may not; many tour players today don't waggle at all, as they feel it complicates the process of settling in at address.

Don't Try to Concentrate for the Entire Round

I don't know if this stems from amateurs watching Jack Nicklaus scowl for eighteen holes on television, stories about

Ben Hogan talking to no one while concentrating steadfastly for eighteen holes, or what. What I know for sure is, too many amateurs try to bear down with no letup for the entire round, usually with disastrous results. Psychological studies have shown it is impossible to concentrate on anything for five solid hours, let alone a taxing pursuit like golf. Attempting to do so will only make you edgy and impatient. In fact, you will concentrate less effectively because you become worn down emotionally, physically, and psychologically.

The best players know that it is important to concentrate intently *only when it counts.* Specifically, this means they start focusing sharply only when they begin the procedure of playing a shot. You cannot be distracted at this time because total concentration is prerequisite to hitting good shots consistently. But after the shot, experienced players soften the intensity of their concentration. How do they accomplish this?

Let's study two players with completely different temperaments—Jack Nicklaus and Lee Trevino. Jack appears to be concentrating all the time. In fact, there have been instances where his good friends have talked to Jack during a round, shaking his hand and wishing him luck, with Jack responding by looking them in the eye and thanking them. After the round, Jack had no recollection of even seeing them. He becomes so deeply immersed in his round that he blocks everything else out. But I can assure you, he is not nearly as deeply focused when he shakes his friends' hands as he is when he is preparing to hit a shot. He spends the rest of the time examining the wind, the condition of the turf, the way the course is playing, how he feels physically, and where he stands in a tournament. It is a passive type of concentration that allows him to save his more intense brand of thinking for when he hits the ball.

Trevino, on the other hand, is always chattering between shots, making jokes, and bantering with the galleries. He doesn't appear to be concentrating at all and in truth he isn't, at least not to the extent that Jack does. But Trevino becomes as intent as Nicklaus the minute he gets over the ball. Watch them and compare. Trevino doesn't talk. Nicklaus doesn't talk. Trevino is concentrating every bit as hard as Jack; he just doesn't do it for

Lee Trevino may talk up a storm in between shots, but once it's his turn to play, he's all business.

as long. Like Jack, Lee focuses in as intensely as possible when he hits a shot, then recedes into a secondary form of concentration that gives his mind a rest.

Learning to focus your concentration at the moment of execution is an essential key to playing well consistently. How you accomplish this depends on your own emotional temperament and concentration span. Experiment—play a round where you don't socialize much. The next round, be a bit more casual and extroverted. See which approach is most productive for you. Chances are, you'll settle for something in between.

You may be puzzled about how not to concentrate between shots. The solution is, let your mind wander a bit. Don't resist the temptation to think about other things while you are walking to your ball. Relax. Ponder the beauty of the course. Engage in light conversation. This will make the game seem a little less serious and will heighten your enjoyment.

When it comes time to hit the shot, however, focus all of your energy on gauging the wind, selecting the right club, visualizing the shot, and making the type of swing that will produce the ball flight you want. If you find it too taxing mentally to go through this process slowly, speed it up. But never take the task of hitting a golf ball lightly.

Expel Negative Thoughts

In most sports, things happen so quickly that the player doesn't have time to dwell on the consequences of his actions. He merely reacts. Sure, there are time-outs in football. In baseball, a relief pitcher has time to contemplate the fact that he's entering the game with the bases loaded. But in golf, you hit only about forty full shots over a five-hour period. That's roughly one shot every eight minutes, which means there's an enormous amount of free time for negative thoughts to creep into your mind. And because amateurs will usually hit at least as many poor shots as good ones, golf by nature tends to encourage more negative thoughts than positive ones.

Managing this part of the game is extremely difficult and

even professionals struggle with it. The fact is, you can't prevent negative thoughts from entering your mind. They may come in the form of feedback after a bad shot, an unlucky bounce, or when an opponent holes a long putt. They really are inescapable. The cure is to form a large umbrella of positive thoughts before the round begins. You need to establish an overall positive mood that is so prevalent that negative thoughts are quickly expelled the moment they occur.

Setting this positive mood requires a little self-trickery. I strongly advocate saying positive things to yourself, even if you don't mean them. "Gosh I feel good today." "I love the feel of these new shoes." "That was a terrific wedge shot I hit on the last hole." "I can't believe how pretty the golf course is this time of year." Such positive statements, whether you mean them or not, have a way of making you feel upbeat and confident. Soon, negative thoughts are in the minority and reduced to insignificance.

There are other tactics you can employ. When you hit a bad shot, make a rule not to be too hard on yourself. If you miss a short putt, don't say to yourself, "What a jerk I am for missing a putt like that." Modify that to, "Come on, Jim. You've practiced accelerating the putter through the ball firmly on those. Let's get on the ball and do it!" In all the years I've spent playing with Jack Nicklaus, the cruellest thing I ever heard him say to himself was, "Oh, Jack!" He knew he could do better and he resolved to give himself a chance to do better. He didn't resign himself to feeling badly about himself or his game.

Dealing with Slow Play

Nothing is more annoying than a four-hour round turning into a five-hour round due to a slow group in front of you. It decreases your enjoyment, tries your patience, breaks your rhythm, allows your concentration to wander, and, ultimately, makes you feel angry. I know. At the Bob Hope Chrysler Classic a couple of years ago, I was shocked to find they had scheduled one of the pro-am rounds at the PGA West Stadium Course,

When my amateur playing partners confronted holes like this at the Bob Hope Chrysler Classic at PGA West, I learned something about coping with slow play.

which may be the hardest course in the world for the high-handicap golfer. The round took about six hours. I was out there trying to play my best, but I was driven to distraction by the constant splashing of balls landing in the water, my playing partners flailing away in the abysslike bunkers, and the interminable waits between my own shots.

This isn't to knock the amateurs. They paid good money to play in the pro-am and they were trying their best. But my poor handling of the situation led me to learn a few things about coping with slow play. I've dealt with it a lot better since.

First of all, the pace of play is out of your hands. It's like getting stuck in traffic. There's nothing you can do about it, so relax. Discuss the stock market. Talk about your families. Tell jokes. Have a soda. When you think about it, what's the alternative—bad golf and more misery? Nobody needs those.

Second, the experience taught me to be more aware of my own pace of play. In my early years, I was an extremely slow

player, mainly due to my desperate situation. I would actually mark my ball on six-inch putts. In retrospect, I can see why this annoyed others in the field. It was thoughtless and inconsiderate. I still am not one of the fastest players on the tour, but I'm not the slowest. And when I began playing faster, I actually played better. No longer am I the last one off the tee when everyone has hit their drives. No longer do I begin lining up putts only when it's my turn to play. I do much of it before. I walk faster to my ball.

If someone in your own group is playing slowly to the point where it's affecting your play, don't hesitate to ask him to speed things up. A lot of players are hesitant to do this, but there's nothing wrong with sauntering over and saying, "Excuse me, but we've got to get moving. Let's be more courteous." Saying something about it is good for two reasons. You'll feel better than if you stewed about it the entire round and you'll also get around the course faster, which solves the problem.

When the Elements Conspire Against You

Golf is played outdoors; consequently, every time a golfer hits the ball he is partly at the mercy of wind, rain, heat, cold, trees, rivers, lakes, mud, sand, and tall grass. The presence of these elements means there is a decided lack of assurance that a good shot will turn out favorably. A perfect drive can roll into a muddy lie. A sudden puff of wind can blow a terrific shot off line just enough to push it into a water hazard. On a rainy day you may make a perfect backswing, only to have a slightly damp grip slip in your hands. A well-struck iron shot may fly directly at the hole, only to hit a hard spot on the green and bounce into tall grass beyond the putting surface.

That's golf, and you had better accept this fact early on. Weather and course conditions are there to conspire against you both mentally and physically. Golf sometimes doesn't seem fair as a result. But as Jack Nicklaus has said, golf wasn't meant to be fair. And, as golf columnist Charles Price said not long ago, serious golf wasn't even meant to be fun, at least not in the whoopee sense in which some approach it.

Dealing with the ungainly task of propelling a ball 1.68 inches in diameter across 500 yards of real estate into a hole 4.25 inches wide through all kinds of weather and turf conditions demands a certain attitude. It requires mental toughness and resiliency to assess this challenge and pursue it with zest, determination, and humility. Many great strikers of the ball have been hindered by their inability to cope with the elements and accept responsibility for the outcome of their shots. I like to think that the best player will win more than others regardless of the conditions. Seve Ballesteros has won tournaments in blazing heat, extreme cold, and in furious downpours. He recognizes that golf is not a lottery but a game of skill, regardless of the conditions.

Beating the elements requires that you be prepared and have a game plan. Not many amateurs take the time to do this, but if you can prepare properly you'll have a tremendous tactical and psychological advantage. Bad weather, you know, eliminates half the field. Here is how to handle various weather conditions.

Cold

At the Bing Crosby tournament at Pebble Beach one year, it actually snowed. At some British Opens, it is so cold that players have to wear three sweaters. Cold presents serious problems, most of them physical. I've learned, however, that preparing properly for cold weather eases the mental strain and frustration of not being able to play your best. Here are some tips:

- *Purchase some hand warmers.* Nothing destroys feel and suppleness in your hands faster than cold. When your fingers are cold, they move more slowly and don't give you accurate feedback when you strike the ball. The slightest mishit can make your hands ring with pain. Hand warmers are the answer. They have saved my kids on hunting trips a hundred times and are excellent for golf. There are two kinds available—the type where you insert a piece of solid fuel into a metal container that slips into a felt pouch and a new type that heats automatically when you remove it from its plastic

Seve Ballesteros has won tournaments worldwide in all types of con-
ditions. His attitude: skill will almost always prevail.

Arnold Palmer (left) *during his Bay Hill tournament—in Florida! Preparation is the key to playing well in cold weather.*

container. They are inexpensive and fit neatly into your pockets.

- *Wear a pair of cart mittens.* Many clubs require members to use a golf cart. A short ride to your ball can make your hands chill very quickly, so I recommend you get a pair of large, boxing-glove-like cart mittens to slip on in between drives to your ball.

- *Wear clothing in layers.* Don't wear a heavy coat, as that restricts body motion during the swing. Instead, put on a T-shirt and then a couple of sweaters. This will keep you almost as warm and yet allows you to swing without being restricted. What's more, you can add or subtract sweaters as the temperature rises or falls. I recommend wool sweaters instead of cotton ones.

  As a corollary to this, you should avoid trying to make long swings. You will be restricted to some extent, and trying to utilize a full range of motion will cause you to lose your balance and hit the ball poorly. And that will play on you mentally.

- *Wear long johns.* Nothing is more important to golf than a good pair of legs, and when they get cold they are not nearly as responsive to motion from your upper body. Long johns are the answer. If you find them to be uncomfortable, try putting on a pair of rain pants over your slacks or trousers. You'll find they are very effective.

- *Wear a stocking cap.* It's a fact that 30 percent of your body heat is lost through your head. Wearing a stocking cap will prevent this loss of energy and also decrease the likelihood of catching a cold. Be sure to cover your ears.

- *Avoid golf carts.* I prefer to walk because the more you move around, the warmer you'll be. Not only will you keep your blood flowing, you'll play better by being able to observe course conditions as you play.

- *Avoid alcohol.* Forget the story about the Saint Bernard delivering brandy to a frozen hiker. Alcohol may make you feel warm, but it's an illusion. Liquor also clouds your thinking.

Heat

Heat is a brutal enemy. I once collapsed at a tournament due to heat prostration. So have many other players. I have since learned that losing body fluids drains you mentally as well as physically. Not only do you lose salt and other vital minerals from your system, which saps your strength, you become impatient and edgy. As your time in the heat increases, you eventually become lethargic and sluggish.

I read recently the Texas Rangers baseball team had discovered their pitching was off by 30 percent during the summer months. A nutrition expert was called in to diagnose the problem, and he found the pitchers were simply getting dehydrated. He suggested they begin drinking a pint of water every inning to combat the problem, and his solution worked. It is now known that soft drinks with high sugar content are counterproductive in hot weather. Water is the best drink in the world. At most PGA Tour events, there is water and/or Gatorade available on every tee. The players demand it, not because they are spoiled but because they know a lack of fluids will have a serious impact on their performance.

Drinking plenty of water at regularly spaced intervals is important. Don't gorge yourself every fourth hole or so. Instead, you should drink a cup on every tee so your fluids are replaced at the same rate at which they are lost. Some other pointers:

- *Watch your pace.* Try to walk at the same speed throughout the round. Not only will this conserve energy, it will help you maintain your inner clock as I described earlier in this chapter.

- *Wear a hat.* Keep your head covered at all times. Direct sunlight will dehydrate you very quickly and can even cause

In warm weather, follow Payne Stewart's example and drink small amounts of water at frequent intervals.

sunstroke. Wear a hat that is well ventilated, so fresh air can circulate near your head.

- *Wear light-colored clothing.* It's been proven that dark colors absorb heat, quickening the pace at which you lose body fluids. Light colors—yellow, white, and light blue—reflect sunlight. I also suggest you wear cotton clothing, as it breathes better than synthetic fabrics and will help you stay cool.

- *Avoid alcohol.* Nothing is more satisfying than a cold beer at the turn. Unfortunately, nothing is more damaging for your game and your health. Instead of restoring body fluids, alcohol depletes them, leaving you susceptible to heat prostration. Drink water instead and save the alcohol for after the round.

- *Avoid the air-conditioned clubhouse.* Going from hot weather to a cold room causes your muscles to stiffen, affecting the suppleness of your swing and increasing the chances of pulling a muscle. At the 1984 PGA Championship at Shoal Creek in Alabama, a rain delay halted play. Lee Trevino, the eventual champion, waited out the delay in the garage of a house alongside the course. Lee knew that if he went indoors, the change in temperature would cause him to tighten up. If you must go indoors, wear a towel over your shoulders.

Rain

Some players are more adept than others at playing in the rain. This is often attributed to their method of swinging the club, but that's only a small part of it. What counts most is their ability to prepare properly and to maintain a positive attitude. Here is how to do it.

- *Keep a rain suit handy.* This may sound obvious, but I'm surprised at how many amateurs are left exposed when it starts to rain while they're on the course. Not only do they get soaking wet, their mental attitude suffers when they re-

Playing in the rain requires preparation and experience. Learn to use your rain gear gracefully so it's an aid, not a distraction.

alize they are unprepared. Look out the window the day you go to play. Listen to the radio, read the newspaper, or watch television. If there's even a slight chance of rain, pack your rain suit.

- *Carry an umbrella—and learn how to use it.* An umbrella can be an invaluable aid, provided you know how to put it to use. I have to laugh when I see amateurs fumbling with their umbrellas. They actually become distracted by them. Some hints: hanging your towel on the wire frame inside the umbrella will help keep the towel dry. Placing your umbrella over your golf clubs when you are hitting a shot will help keep your clubs dry. Using an umbrella while driving a golf cart is awkward and distracting. Sometimes it is better to rely on your rain suit and a hat to keep you as dry as possible.

- *Keep your grips dry.* Nothing is worse than swinging a wet, slippery club. You have no control. Even when the club doesn't slip in your hands, the fear that it will prevents you from concentrating solely on hitting the ball. The solution is

to bring an extra towel or two so you can wipe your grips dry before every shot. And because your hands are the only part of your body that touches the club, make sure you keep them dry as well. If you wear a golf glove, bring a couple of extra pairs and store them in a plastic bag.

- *Bring a change of clothing.* I can't tell you what a lift I get when I'm able to put on a pair of fresh socks at the turn, while my opponent has to play the rest of the way wearing the same, soggy pair. Also keep a fresh shirt and spare pair of shoes in your locker. Remember, preparation is everything.

- *Carry a rule book.* Rain changes the condition of the golf course and, consequently, provokes a lot of rules situations. Do you know how to take relief from casual water? What *is* casual water? What do you do if your ball comes to rest in an area where water has spilled outside the margin of a hazard? In competition, is there a lift, clean, and drop rule in effect? Are you granted relief for an embedded ball anywhere through the green or in the fairway only?

  Always carry a rule book. Learn how to proceed in every circumstance. This is especially important in competition, where the rules are strictly enforced. Inquire about any local rules that may be in effect for the tournament.

- *Never give up.* On extremely rainy days, players invariably shoot a higher score for the first nine holes than they expected. The tendency is to give up. I love this kind of scenario, because I know that on the back nine I have a huge advantage over most of the field simply because I have resolved to make the most of the bad conditions. Now is the time to suck in your belly and play golf. Be patient. Play the percentages. Take the course and weather conditions in stride.

Wind

As the television announcer and former PGA champion Dave Marr has said, rain doesn't drive scores up nearly as

A typical sight in Britain, where windy conditions are the norm. Patience, concentration, and imagination are vital in this type of weather.

quickly as wind. At the Honda Classic in 1986, Kenny Knox shot an 80 in the windswept third round and still won the tournament. The Scots like to say, "If there's nae wind there's nae golf," and looking on this part of nature as a challenge instead of a hindrance is a secret to playing well.

Attitude is important here. There is more to mastering the wind than learning the type of swing mechanics that will enable you to hit the ball so the wind doesn't affect it. The key is to plan your strategy for each hole before you tee off so you don't have to strain your mind on every shot. Some things to consider follow.

- *Which holes will play into the wind? Which will play downwind?* A stiff breeze in your face may make some par 4s unreachable in two shots. Accept this and plan your strategy accordingly. Since you can't reach the green in two anyway, maybe use a 2-iron off the tee if the fairway is narrow, so as

to keep the ball in play. Once you make your strategy, don't deviate from it unless absolutely necessary.

• *Practice hitting balls in the wind.* Which should you do: draw the ball into a left-to-right crosswind (Sam Snead's method) or hit a fade so the ball curves in the direction the wind is blowing (Jack Nicklaus's method)? How far can you hit each club into a head wind? Opinions on such questions vary. The only way to find out is by practicing when it's windy.

• *Practice putting in the wind.* If you are slight of build, as I once was, the biggest peril of playing in the wind may be putting. A gust of wind can knock you off balance and make you push or pull the putt. There are three answers here: technique, patience, and concentration. You may need to develop a secondary putting technique that provides you with more stability in the wind. Do this by widening your stance and perhaps bending over closer to the ball. As for patience, don't hit a putt quickly in between gusts of wind just to avoid being blown off balance. Take your time and don't putt until you're ready. The same applies for concentration. Don't allow the wind whistling in your ears to break your concentration. Stay single-minded about making the putt and don't rush.

Is Golf a Social Game or a Competitive One?

People play golf for many reasons. Some prefer the camaraderie, companionship, and conversation that is part of the game. Some love the fresh air and exercise. Others simply use the game as a means of getting out of the office or out of the house on weekends. These things are part and parcel of the game. For many serious golfers, however, the social demands of golf can be distracting and can prevent you from playing your best.

My demeanor on and off the golf course has always been similar to Dr. Jekyll and Mr. Hyde. It concerned me for a long time. Off the course I'm relaxed and enjoy the company of

friends and family. On the course, I'm quiet, stern, and reclusive, which I feel is necessary to play my best. This behavior is accepted in the world of professional golf. The question is, is it acceptable for you in the social environment of a golf club? Can you afford to project the wrong impression of your true personality to your playing partners, even though you know it will help you play better? Should you be more relaxed and talkative? These questions need answering, because worrying about how others perceive you on the golf course can directly influence your play.

More than any other game, golf demands that you absorb yourself into it completely. The balance between the physical and mental sides of the game is delicate and requires full attention almost all of the time. Serious golfers understand this. Tour pros may talk and smile to the gallery as they stand on the tee, but seldom do they talk up a storm all the way up the fairway. They are too busy plotting strategy, noting changes in the wind, assessing a way to play their next shot, or engaging in other forms of thought.

If your primary motivation for playing is to tell jokes and laugh about the funny shank you just hit, fine. There's nothing wrong with that. But if you are out there to shoot a good score and improve your game, and feel you can do it best by talking little, seek out playing partners who are the same way. Don't set up a weekend game with the club's rowdiest group and then resent their behavior and attitude. You'll only play worse and gain a reputation for being a spoilsport.

There are other nuances about the social game of golf. Here are some, with my suggestions for handling them.

- *If one of your playing partners is having a bad day,* be sympathetic. Say a nice word or two on occasion. But for the most part leave him alone. Don't exacerbate his misery or allow yourself to be dragged into his mood. Bad attitudes are contagious, so concentrate on your own game.

- *If you are paired with someone who has a bad temper,* avoid him. Walk up the other side of the fairway. Don't get close

Curtis Strange and Jay Haas enjoy a few laughs on the tee. Their so-cial banter, however, stops when it's time to hit shots.

to him. Talk to him after the round, but don't allow him to upset your inner rhythm and concentration.

- *If you are having a bad day,* be considerate. If you feel like complaining about the speed of the greens or the new sand in the bunkers, do it tactfully. Don't drag others into the frustration you may be feeling.

- *If you are paired with an incessant talker or complainer,* humor him while at the same time shutting him out. This can be done, you know. Listening never hurt anybody, but don't listen so closely that you are distracted from the matter at hand.

Summary

In this chapter we have explored why golf is more difficult than other games, and I have offered practical advice on handling some of the unique problems it presents. I thought it wise to include this information early on. No matter how far you progress in golf, these problems will continue to present a special challenge to your skill and spirit.

To this point, most of my advice has been of a hands-on nature. But as we will see, the truly tough competitor also utilizes a constellation of mental skills to combat these and other problems.

3

The Elements of Mental Toughness

What Great Players Have in Common

After my career in golf really took off when I came to America in the early 1970s, I sometimes wondered what happened to players I had seen and known in Australia and on the Asian Tour. I couldn't figure out why they hadn't had the success I'd had. Many of them were far more talented than I, and in my early years, one of my greatest sources of discouragement was wondering how I could possibly succeed against players who were bigger and stronger, hit the ball farther, putted better, had access to great teachers, and generally had all the positive attributes I didn't.

One of these fellows was an Australian named Bob Stanton. He was an incredible striker of the ball and possessed the best swing I had seen to that point in my career. If ever there was a can't-miss prospect, it was Bob Stanton. Among other accomplishments, he beat Arnold Palmer in a play-off at the Dunlop International when Palmer was in his prime. In Australia, Stanton was widely regarded by the press and his peers as the next superstar in golf.

Stanton eventually made his way to the U.S., where he had some mediocre success. Before long, however, people were asking, "Whatever happened to Bob Stanton?" He all but disappeared from competitive golf and today is putting together corporate golf packages.

A similar story concerns Eddie Pearce. At age sixteen, he won the U.S. Junior Amateur. At eighteen, he won the Florida Open. At nineteen, he was runner-up in the U.S. Amateur. When Pearce left Wake Forest University for the PGA Tour, some thought he already was one of the best players in the game.

Pearce had unbelievable talent. He could, and did, use his driver on some fairway bunker shots, a feat that requires exquisite hand-eye coordination. He could hit the ball for incredible distances, yet also had the touch of someone who defuses bombs for a living. During his first month on the tour, he finished second in the Hawaiian Open. Within a few years, however, Eddie Pearce was off the tour. It was hard to believe, really, that a player with that much innate ability could fail to accomplish great things.

Examples like these—and there are hundreds of them—mystified me for a long time. What could have held them back? The answer is more clear to me now. This is not to criticize Bob Stanton or Eddie Pearce in any way, *but they did not have all of the attributes necessary to succeed in golf.* It may have been that they disliked the grind of traveling and living out of a suitcase. Maybe they found other endeavors in life more rewarding. There is nothing wrong with that. But in any case, they came up short in one or two vital areas that were necessary if they were to achieve the success their talent warranted.

Attaining excellence in golf, or any athletic endeavor, requires control over a defined set of mental skills that I will outline in this chapter. As we shall see, a profound weakness in any of these areas will keep a professional off the tour and will prevent the amateur from realizing his full potential. Once these skills are identified and addressed effectively, however, you will acquire the most elusive elements in golf: mental toughness and consistency.

Consistency: the Final Payoff

In the Golf Digest instruction schools, amateur students are given a questionnaire in which they are asked their number-one goal in golf. The most common answer: consistency. Simply de-

Eddie Pearce, a phenomenal golfer with immense physical skills, lacked some of the psychological traits necessary to succeed at the highest levels of the game.

fined, consistency means performing near the upper range of your skills on a regular basis. Golf is by far the most difficult sport to be consistent at. Playing at your peak on a regular basis is extremely difficult for pros and amateurs.

The search for consistency is maddening. Why do you play well one day and poorly the next? How can you have good rhythm and tempo one day and almost none twenty-four hours later? Why does your swing alternate between feeling good and

bad? How is it possible to practice hitting your driver every day for the week prior to an important tournament, then, with the problem seemingly ironed out, proceed to hit your tee shots crooked when the event begins? How can you "hole everything" with the putter one round and then miss several four-footers the next?

Inconsistency stems from an inability to master the set of mental skills I am talking about. The struggle to be consistent is a source of tremendous frustration for all golfers, amateurs especially. It is no fun to sacrifice time and to devote a great deal of effort and thought to your golf game, only to play poorly when it counts. It brings on self-doubt, anger, resignation, and despair. It takes the fun out of the game, because the greatest pleasure comes from improving and playing well when you want to most. It is a fact that many golfers quit trying to improve when they experience these feelings, simply because their effort isn't paying off.

Achieving consistency is the ultimate measure of mental toughness and, as I see it, is the trademark of every great player in history. To wit:

- Jack Nicklaus won major championships twenty-seven years apart and had an unbelievable career in between. That's consistency.

- Gary Player has won 135 tournaments around the world since the late 1950s and in 1988 won the U.S. Senior Open. That's consistency.

- Sam Snead won his first Greensboro Open in 1938, his last in 1965. He won eighty-two PGA Tour events in between. That's consistency.

- Tom Kite has been among the top-ten money winners on the PGA Tour for eight of the last nine years. That's consistency.

Consistency embraces two elements. The first is good technique and form. You must work on building sound swing

Few golfers in history have been as consistent as Tom Kite. A dedicated, thoughtful student of the game, Kite's steadiness is due in part to his tremendous self-control.

mechanics and learn the nuances of putting and the short game if you are to play well day in and day out. The second is good mental skills, which are at least as important. Consistency is important in thought as well as in deed, and you must be able to control your thought processes, attitudes, and emotions on the course if you are to take your game to a higher level.

Defining the Necessary Mental Skills

All great players in history have achieved mental toughness and consistency through the display of a defined set of mental skills. These players have been:

1. Self-motivated

2. Positive but realistic

3. In control of their emotions

4. Calm and relaxed under fire

5. Highly energetic and ready for action

6. Determined

7. Mentally alert

8. Doggedly self-confident

9. Fully responsible

It is important to realize that these skills are learned, not inherited. In my early years I displayed very few of them and only came to learn them informally through trial and error. I could not have identified them even eight years ago, although by that point I had become proficient enough in all areas to have won the PGA Championship and U.S. Open. I don't think I could have identified them as concretely as I can now. Today, these mental skills are very sharp and real to me and I am convinced they can be put to use by anyone, regardless of individual personality, temperament, or physical ability.

As I describe each of these skills, evaluate how you rate in each area. Make note of where you need the most improvement (you may need help in *all* areas) so you can devote more energy to solving that problem.

1. *Self-motivated.* Above all else, golf is an individual game. There are no coaches telling you how much time you need to practice. There are no teammates you'll let down with a poor performance. No one tells you how to regulate your life. The amateur who aspires to improve his game and compete success-fully determines how much time he devotes to hitting balls, the extent to which he'll sacrifice other areas of personal enjoyment on behalf of golf, how much money he spends on lessons and equipment, and so on. Your motivation must come from within, and the intensity of that motivation is determined by how badly you want to perform well.

On the PGA Tour, where I make most of my living, golf is radically different than other forms of work. There is no time clock to punch. No one tells the players what foods to eat or what time we must go to bed. Yet, pro golfers are some of the most disciplined athletes in the world.

Ben Hogan may have been the most disciplined golfer of all. As he neared the end of his playing career, he accepted an invi-tation to play in the Westchester Classic in New York. Ben's left leg, injured in a terrible automobile accident in 1949, was giving him a lot of trouble. Unfortunately, he was given an early tee time and in order to get himself ready to play, he found it nec-essary to rise at about 4:00 A.M. He had to soak and wrap his bad leg just so he could walk the course. Now, Hogan was very secure financially, and if anyone had nothing left to prove in golf, it was he. But he was motivated by a desire to play well, and it took tremendous self-discipline to arise at that awful hour to do so.

Hogan showed this self-motivation and self-direction much earlier in his career. Not many people know that Hogan turned professional in 1928 at the age of sixteen. Several times he ven-tured onto the pro tour, only to return home broke and discour-

The great Ben Hogan was one of the most highly motivated athletes of all time. Pride and an intense desire to master his craft led Hogan to practice as much as twelve hours per day.

aged. It took eighteen years of sacrifice, hard financial times, and incredible willpower before he finally won his first major championship, the 1946 PGA Championship. It was self-motivation that saw him through.

Obviously, few amateurs have in mind the lofty goals Ben Hogan had. But whatever your aspirations, whether it's first place in the D flight of your club championship or to qualify for your state amateur, it is self-motivation that will produce the effort necessary for you to reach your goal.

How can you increase your self-motivation? My biggest strength is my family. It is enormously helpful to have a support system at home or among close friends. Encouragement and support from outside sources provides extra incentive and will help you summon extra strength to reach your goals.

*There was no containing my elation when I holed the final putt to win
the 1980 Memorial tournament. Until that moment, however, I kept my
emotions under control.*

Here are some other tips. Try them and see if they inspire you to work hard.

- *Think back to a situation where you failed.* Although you don't want to dwell on negative experiences very often or for very long, reliving a moment of failure can make you work extremely hard to avoid experiencing that feeling again. In most situations where a player performs poorly, he knows it was his own lack of preparation or bad thinking that led to the setback. On the PGA Tour, a player who hits a poor shot on the last hole can very often be found on the practice range after the round, doggedly working on the shot that let him down so he won't make the same mistake again.

- *Think back to a moment of triumph.* Remember the sensation of shooting your best round ever or winning your first tournament? As you well know, there is no feeling quite like it. Close your eyes and try to remember every wonderful moment of it. Many athletes will work for years just to experience that moment again.

- *Remember, there is no time to waste.* Keep in mind that while you lay on the couch at home, other serious golfers are out working on their games and improving. You can't afford to let time stand still. Knowledge of that fact should gnaw at you until you do something about it.

- *Set goals with your practice and don't leave until you reach them.* Gary Player used to practice hitting greenside bunker shots until he holed five or more. Sometimes it took him hours, but he stayed there until he did it. When Ken Green used to practice at his home course, he would sometimes leave a five-dollar bill in the putting cup when he didn't reach the personal goal he had set for himself. This type of motivation is extremely effective.

- *Purchase a videotape of your favorite pro winning a tournament.* It will give you a vicarious thrill and inspire you to practice. Watching Curtis Strange win the U.S. Open will

Gary Player has said that the word impossible does not exist in his vocabulary. He is always energetic, optimistic, and ready to give it his all.

make your personal goal, such as winning the club championship, seem more attainable by comparison.

The bottom line is, anything you can do to increase your self-motivation is good.

2. *Positive but realistic.* Every golfer has limitations, yet the good ones are not discouraged by the things they cannot do. They focus instead on the things they can do and look to these strengths for confidence, inspiration, and encouragement.

A terrific example is Jerry Barber, who at five feet, five inches may be the shortest golfer ever to win a major title. When Barber won the 1961 PGA Championship in a play-off against Don January, little Jerry was outdriven on virtually every hole and in many cases had to use fairway woods to reach the par-4 holes. Barber, however, is one of the greatest chippers and putters in history and knows it. He wasn't intimidated at being outdriven by January. Although the temptation for him to get a little extra distance off the tee had to be immense as they played the final holes, Barber remained poised and realistic about his shortness off the tee. He never pressed, never tried a shot he wasn't capable of executing. Still, he remained extremely positive about winning, confident in the fact that his short game would keep him in contention.

Barber's approach paid off even before the play-off began. On the seventieth hole of the championship proper, he made a twenty-foot putt for a birdie. On the seventy-first, he sank a forty-footer for another birdie. On the final hole, Barber drilled a sixty-foot putt to tie January. In the eighteen-hole play-off the following day, Barber chipped and putted tremendously and shot a 67 to January's 68.

Paul Runyan, who was nicknamed "Little Poison" because of his small stature, is another extremely positive person who is realistic about his limitations off the tee. In the final of the 1938 PGA Championship, then contested at match play, Runyan was regularly outdriven by Sam Snead, sometimes by as much as forty yards. But Paul made up for it with incredible play on and

Jerry Barber has had phenomenal success despite standing only five feet, five inches. A short hitter, he always plays within his capabilities.

around the greens. He won the match and the title by the incredible margin of 8 and 7.

If you are a short hitter, a poor bunker player, or struggle with the fairway woods, don't push your luck in those areas, especially in competition. You're sure to hit poor shots and will become frustrated and discouraged. Instead, recognize your shortcomings and don't attempt shots you have very little chance of executing. If you fade the ball, don't gamble with a high hook. If you are a poor sand player, aim for the fat part of the green on bunker shots. If you don't trust your fairway woods, use an iron for your second shot on par 5s. Play within your capabilities, be patient, and take heart in the fact that there are many ways to beat an opponent.

3. *In control of their emotions.* You doubtless know the adverse effects of emotional blowups. Becoming upset by bad rulings,

silly mistakes, annoying playing partners, poor playing conditions, or bad breaks will, in almost every case, have an adverse effect on your physical performance. Mentally tough golfers have thick skins and don't let outside circumstances influence their play. They know that if a player doesn't control his emotions, his emotions will control him.

In the 1970 World Cup, which Bruce Devlin and I won for Australia, I learned a valuable lesson about emotional control. I played extremely well and, with rounds of 65-67-65, was in the hunt for the individual title as the fourth round began. The World Cup that year was held in Buenos Aires, Argentina, and the raucous gallery was doing everything it could to ensure that their Argentine hero, Roberto De Vicenzo, win the individual trophy. Crowd control was terrible. I'd hit a good drive and Roberto would hit a poor one, but when we walked down the fairway I'd find my ball in the rough and Roberto's in the fairway. On one hole Roberto blew his approach shot over the bleachers behind the green, but when we got to the green there was Roberto's ball, twenty feet from the hole. It was almost more than I could handle emotionally and, in fact, I played rather poorly, shooting a 73 to finish second to Roberto by one stroke.

I was extremely upset, but I noticed that my teammate, Devlin, had remained perfectly poised through it all. He realized there was nothing we could do about it and he just played his game. He handled the situation better than I, and when it was all over, I vowed not to let my emotions get out of control again. There was no question that my being upset probably accounted for that one-stroke margin of defeat.

Don't feel victimized by bad breaks. The moment you start feeling sorry for yourself, you're looking for an excuse to lose. There are many, many players who let fear and anger stand in their way. Put yourself above all of it and be ready to accept the consequences, good or bad.

4. *Calm and relaxed under fire.* Great players are at their very best when the heat is on. They don't avoid pressure; they are challenged by it. Jack Nicklaus is a terrific example. When

Roberto De Vicenzo certainly had the crowd on his side during the 1970 World Cup. I learned a valuable lesson in self-control from that experience.

Nicklaus came to the 1986 Masters Tournament, he was forty-six years old and had not won a PGA Tour event in two years. He had putted poorly (for him), had difficulty motivating himself, and had decreased his schedule of tournaments. The press had even questioned Jack's ability to handle pressure situations.

As Nicklaus came to the ninth hole of the final round, he was even par for the day and six shots behind the leader, Seve Ballesteros. Jack birdied the ninth. Then he birdied the tenth and eleventh. The odds were still against him and the pressure was mounting steadily, but Nicklaus didn't back off. He became energized and suddenly got a gleam in his eye that seemed to say, "I want the pressure." Jack bogeyed the twelfth hole, but he then birdied the thirteenth, parred the fourteenth, *eagled* the fifteenth, birdied the sixteenth, birdied the seventeenth, and very nearly birdied the eighteenth. Jack won that Masters, the sixth of his career.

As Jack played the back nine, his adrenaline was pumping, tears of emotion welled in his eyes, and the galleries were screaming. The situation would have unnerved many golfers, but Nicklaus never let it adversely affect his game. He remained calm and relaxed enough to think and act clearly and decisively. He made the pressure work for him or at least prevented it from working against him.

This trait may be the most difficult of all for the average player to learn. It is extremely hard for the amateur to maintain his composure under pressure, simply because he isn't in pressure situations very often. I'll be frank: there are no shortcuts to mastering this. You have to be under fire a few times before you can feel calm and relaxed under fire. Seek out pressure situations. Play in more tournaments. Maybe increase the size of your wagers in your weekend games. Offer to play two shots lower than your handicap. Arrange games with players better than you. Seek out the best teacher in your area.

5. *Highly energetic and ready for action.* Top professionals are capable of getting themselves pumped up and energized to play well regardless of the circumstances. They may be fatigued, injured, hopelessly behind in a tournament, or beset by personal

In 1986, Jack Nicklaus completed a round of 65 to win his sixth Masters title. Nicklaus hadn't contended in a major championship for years, yet he maintained his poise beautifully.

problems, yet they never quit. They find a way to approach every round of golf with enthusiasm and determination.

At the 1988 British Open at Royal Lytham and St. Anne's, Curtis Strange arrived physically tired from a grueling schedule of tournaments and emotionally drained from the excitement of winning the U.S. Open a month earlier. On top of this, he was feeling the effects of jet lag. He shot a miserable 80 in the first round, which all but made it impossible for him to win the championship. Some players would have felt the urge to turn in a mediocre effort the next day, miss the cut, and take the next plane home. Not Curtis. He got some rest, thought about the next round, and prepared to give it all he had. The result: Curtis shot a 69 in the second round, made the cut, and added rounds of 69 and 68, giving himself a very respectable thirteenth-place finish.

The question is, was it worth trying so hard just to finish thirteenth? The answer is an unequivocal yes. Having the pride and optimism to give it your very best in difficult situations makes it that much easier to succeed in all circumstances. Curtis Strange knows, as do all top competitors, that success requires an indefatigable spirit and determination to approach every situation with enthusiasm, zeal, and optimism.

Gary Player is much the same way. In the 1978 Masters, Gary began the final round seven strokes behind the leader, Hubert Green. Most players in his position would have considered themselves out of contention, but not Gary. He actually thought he had a very good chance of winning. He birdied seven of the last ten holes, tied the course record with a 64, and won his third green coat. He was so energized by the vague prospect of winning that he actually began running toward the par-5 fifteenth green after reaching it in two shots.

Was Gary Player energetic? You bet. Was he ready for action? No doubt about it. You will find that, by adopting a similar attitude, success will come more easily and frequently than you thought possible.

6. *Determined.* There are instances where I've been behind in a tournament and been asked by the press about my chances of

winning. In some cases I've avoided expressing my true feelings because my words would be construed as being boastful. Professionals, however, speak confidently to each other about their intentions and goals because we know we aren't boasting. Outsiders can't relate to the professional's determination, his sheer force of will that makes seemingly impossible tasks possible. Determination is one of the biggest differences between winners and losers, pros and amateurs, success and failure.

Greg Norman provides a perfect example. At the 1988 Australian PGA at Riverside Oaks, Greg opened with a mediocre 75, which left him nine strokes out of the lead. As Greg and I flew back into the city that night, he turned to me and said, "If I play half decently, I can shoot 62 on that golf course." I was a little surprised. I mean, Riverside Oaks is not an easy course. I didn't say anything to Greg, just nodded. The next day, Norman shot 64. Unfortunately for Greg, he wound up losing the tournament in a play-off, but I later wondered how the press would have responded to Greg's assertion that he could shoot 62. They probably would have made him sound boastful, but, in fact, Greg wasn't boasting. He was simply determined to do better, and he very nearly reached his goal.

Norman showed the same determination at the ESP Open at Royal Canberra. This time, he didn't keep his intentions secret. After carding a 62 in the opening round, Greg stomped into the press tent and said, "I am really hot right now. I should have broken 60 today." The press couldn't believe that Norman was upset about shooting 62, but Greg really felt he should have shot 59 or better. And with that kind of determination, it is very likely that Greg will someday do it.

Determined individuals are hard to beat. They set goals that others view as unreachable, and they don't give up until they achieve them. Setbacks are taken in stride. When Larry Mize chipped in to beat Greg Norman at the 1987 Masters, and when Bob Tway holed a bunker shot on the final hole to beat Greg at the 1986 PGA Championship, Greg responded by trying even harder. Adopt just a piece of that determination, and nothing can stand in your way.

7. *Mentally alert.* The best golfers have the ability to tune in what's important and tune out that which is not. They are selective about what they see and hear and only take in data that is pertinent to the task at hand. They are aware of everything going on around them, but they weed out everything that is negative or incidental.

In the final round of the 1975 Masters, Jack Nicklaus faced a forty-foot putt on the sixteenth green that would tie him for the lead with Tom Weiskopf. Incredibly, Jack sank the putt and went on to win the tournament. When asked about the putt after the round, Jack said he knew how the putt would break because he'd had a similar putt on the same green several years earlier— *several years earlier.* Jack was so alert, so focused, that he was able to recall a tiny detail about something that had happened long ago. Moreover, he could recall that detail while under enormous pressure.

Alertness and presence of mind are vitally important in golf, yet they are often overlooked. The game is played at such a leisurely pace and is so relaxing that many amateurs drift into a hazy state of mind where they aren't aware of things that could help them during play. For instance, while playing the tenth hole, do you ever look over to the sixteenth green to see where the flagstick is located? Do you pay close attention to how your playing partner's ball behaves when it lands on the green, so you can determine whether the green is hard or soft?

Lack of alertness even hurts professionals. Johnny Miller was once disqualified from a tournament because he had inadvertently put his son's cut-down putter in his bag and failed to notice it before he teed off. The rules allow fourteen clubs; Johnny had fifteen. In the 1989 Tournament of Champions, Arnold Palmer was penalized for hitting from the wrong tees. On the final hole of a play-off for the 1955 U.S. Open, Ben Hogan failed to clean his spikes before he hit his last drive of the day, slipped during his swing, and hit a duck hook that ruined his chance at winning.

By being alert, you diminish the chances of making silly mistakes. You'll swing the club better because you're more in tune

with your physical being. In tournaments, you'll notice many of the little things other amateurs tend to overlook.

8. *Doggedly self-confident.* Every champion has a deep, unwavering belief in himself and his ability to perform well. This self-confidence is almost indestructible and is unaffected by what others say or do. Supremely self-confident people are resilient to setbacks, can shrug off pressure, and are not easily intimidated. On the other hand, when a golfer has high self-confidence, he can appear intimidating to others.

Seve Ballesteros possesses an intangible quality that golf fans call charisma. He has a presence about him, a certain bearing that sets him apart from ordinary individuals. I think this charisma stems from his enormous self-confidence. On the golf course, Seve's extraordinary self-assurance can be intimidating to others. Jack Nicklaus is intimidating in the same way. Neither player tries to intimidate others; they simply do because of the way they carry themselves and the way they play golf.

Years ago, Arnold Palmer was a paragon of self-confidence. He had—and still has—a bold, go-for-broke style of play. He loved to gamble on par 5s, was an extremely aggressive putter, and usually chose to slash his way out of trouble rather than accept a penalty stroke. It was a style that demanded self-confidence, because one shred of doubt is all it takes to turn a gambling shot into a disastrous one. Most of the time Arnold's style paid off, and he has a U.S. Open, four Masters, and two British Open titles to prove it.

Developing self-confidence is critical, for many other attributes follow in its wake. Self-confident people are also proud, motivated, upbeat, and unafraid of success. They find it easier to summon the courage to attempt challenges others shy away from.

9. *Fully responsible.* Because golf is an individual game, it is important that you learn to take responsibility for your own actions. Every great golfer has done this. They don't make excuses and they don't blame others for their failures. They realize their

Arnold Palmer's gambling style of golf was predicated on enormous self-confidence.

destiny is in their own hands, and they rely on themselves for the strength necessary to succeed.

When Jack Nicklaus lost the 1977 British Open to Tom Watson, Nicklaus got up at the presentation ceremony, turned to Watson, and said, "I gave it my best shot and it wasn't good enough. You were better." Jack gave full credit to Watson and accepted responsibility for his losing performance. There was no moaning from Jack about Watson holing a sixty-foot putt from the fringe of the sixteenth hole or of the boisterous crowd that sometimes distracted Nicklaus by venturing onto the fairways. He lost the tournament and was willing to accept the consequences.

I received a stern lesson in this area in the 1985 British Open at Royal St. George's. I was near the lead as I stood on the fifteenth tee. I hit a super drive, but the ball hit a mound in the fairway and kicked sideways into a horrible little bunker from where I made a bogey. Golf is inherently unfair sometimes and I was plenty upset, but I bit my lip and accepted the fact that I was the one who hit the shot and I would have to accept the consequences. There is no sense in feeling victimized or cursed with bad luck. It only breeds self-pity and a losing attitude.

When you learn responsibility, you become tougher and more resilient to misfortune. You become more self-reliant and take precautions against making decisions that will hurt you.

4

The Power of the "Zone"
A Magical State of Mind

People assume that my winning the 1981 U.S. Open at Merion Golf Club was the most memorable achievement of my career. That isn't completely true. Certainly it was the most important tournament I ever won, the most thrilling, the most rewarding. But "memorable" isn't completely accurate, because I have difficulty recalling some of the details of that warm June day when I shot a 68 to produce what Bob Rosburg and others have called "one of the great rounds in U.S. Open history."

Not long after I finished the round, I was surprised to learn I had hit every green in regulation (actually I was on the fringe of three greens but used my putter) and had missed only one fairway with my tee shots. I had no idea I had played that well. I vaguely remember talking with my caddie, but I don't recall what was said. I have to look at films of the tournament to refresh my memory as to where flagsticks were located on some of the greens. I've been intrigued with this short-term memory loss ever since. On a day where I probably should remember everything, I have trouble reconstructing what happened from the first tee on.

I have since learned that on that day I entered what is known as the "Zone" or the "Bubble." It is a state of mind close to being hypnotized, where everything takes on a dreamy, tranquil quality and you are in complete control of your mind and body. I am not the first golfer to experience it. Author Dan Jenkins refers to the "coma" Jack Fleck was in when he won the 1955 U.S. Open in an eighteen-hole play-off against Ben Hogan.

I was clearly in the Zone when I captured the 1976 Westchester Classic.

Al Geiberger after shooting an incredible 59 to win the 1977 Memphis Classic. It took Geiberger some time to realize what he had accomplished.

Fleck, an obscure driving range pro from Iowa, seemed not at all nervous as he birdied the seventy-second hole to get into the play-off. After having a full evening to ponder what winning the U.S. Open could do for his life and career, Fleck performed in the play-off without a hint of intimidation, fear, or anxiety. Al Geiberger, who shot an incredible score of 59 in the 1977 Memphis Classic, recalls that after he holed his final birdie putt on the last green, "I didn't realize at the moment exactly what I had done. . . I only realized the enormity of it when I walked into the press room and got a long, standing ovation. It wasn't until I came out of my daze that I began to appreciate my accomplishment."

The Zone is not the exclusive territory of professionals. You doubtless have seen your amateur friends have days where they are "unconscious" with the putter or perform far above their usual ability from tee to green. You probably have experienced the eerie sensation of knowing you were going to hole a putt before you made the stroke. Or days where you inexplicably hit the ball ten yards farther with every club, even though it felt as though you were swinging in slow motion with minimal effort. Just think how good you could be if you performed like that all the time!

For me, golf was never easier than it was that last day of the 1981 Open. I was oblivious to the tremendous pressure I was under. I did not think for a moment of the consequences of a poor shot. There was no fussing over the technical details of my swing. I was almost completely unaware of the thousands of people in the gallery, of the television cameras watching my every move, of the competitors making a run to overtake me. Mentally and physically, it was as though I were on automatic pilot. My thoughts were clear, ordered, and decisive. All I did was pull a club from the bag, swing, and the type of shot I envisioned would come off perfectly.

Needless to say, I tried my utmost to recapture that unique mental state in every subsequent round I played. It proved to be an elusive, frustrating task. The chief problem was trying to identify the elements of that special mind-set so I could try to

Only after I held the 1981 U.S. Open trophy in my hands did I emerge from the peculiar mental state that allowed me to win it.

incorporate them into my mental makeup during competition. My inability to do this made it impossible for me to get into the Zone when I wanted to most. Naturally, a good deal of frustration followed. But just when I was about to resign myself to the fact that no one could capture this mystical state deliberately, I would wander into the Zone again by accident, playing tremendous golf with no conscious effort. For no apparent reason, the club would suddenly feel firm and comfortable in my hands. The green would appear more sharply focused as I was about to make an approach shot. I could "see" an extremely clear line to

the hole when I stood over a putt. My senses of sight, sound, vision, and even smell would become highly acute. I could almost hear my heart beating. Emotionally, nothing would upset me.

Since those days I have learned more about this ideal performance state and how you can attain it. I am convinced that learning to control it is the key to playing well consistently, because all physical action is rooted in the mind. If you can identify, understand, and control the psychological factors that influence your performance, your physical execution will improve.

Concretely identifying those psychological factors has been one of the great challenges of modern sport. Thanks to the work of athletes and sports psychologists, we now know what they are, why they are important, and how they interact when we perform. Ultimately, we are able to quantify the Zone and provide practical instruction on how it can be acquired and put to use.

In chapter 3, I described the elements of mental toughness. For the most part, those elements are a by-product of the ideal performance state and will occur naturally when you learn to get into the Zone. The characteristics of the Zone are unique and require a different method of application, as we will later see.

For now, we will identify the eleven elements of the Zone and examine them individually. We'll discuss ways you can improve your performance in each. In chapter 5, we'll address the process of putting all of these elements together so all are working for you at once.

Here are the eleven elements of the Zone and their basic characteristics.

1. *Mental calmness*. At all times you should feel a sense of quiet and calm inside, regardless of what goes on around you. Only then are you in total control of your mind and body.

2. *Physical relaxation*. Golfers perform best when they are feeling loose, with minimal muscle tension. You should feel relaxed, fluid, and ready for action.

3. *Low anxiety*. Your ability to function in the present, without thought to what has already happened or what lies ahead, determines how effectively you think and behave.

4. *Energy*. Incorporating the high-positive type of energy into your mental makeup leads to a more alert, zestful, productive physical performance.

5. *Optimism*. When you think good things are about to happen, good things usually will happen. If you can see the glass as half-full as opposed to half-empty, your enjoyment increases and so does your capacity to play well.

6. *Enjoyment*. If you can make golf a fun, enjoyable pastime, even under serious competitive conditions, you'll play better.

7. *Effortless*. If you can think and perform with a minimum of conscious thought, your body will react with maximum efficiency.

8. *Automatic*. Instilling and maintaining the right inner rhythm under all conditions is prerequisite to consistently high performance.

9. *Alertness*. Being totally aware of all that goes on in the golf environment ensures that all meaningful factors are taken into account before you swing the club.

10. *Self-confidence*. When you believe in yourself, you are more calm and poised in every situation. Though self-confidence cannot be manufactured, it can be cultivated.

11. *In control*. Taking charge of the situation, rather than letting the situation control you, is a hallmark of every champion. Controlling your emotions regardless of what happens leads to psychological stability and more physical control.

Let's look at each of these elements individually and discuss ways you can improve in each one.

Mental Calmness

In the fall of 1988, I witnessed an incident during a pro-am in Springfield, Missouri, that to me underscored the importance of a calm state of mind. One of my amateur partners was a nice, unassuming fellow who understandably felt a little nervous at the prospect of playing with a professional for the first time. Frankly, I didn't think much of it because I've played in hundreds of pro-ams and am used to seeing the amateurs relax a little after we shake hands and chat a bit.

This guy was different. He seemed to get more nervous as our tee time approached. When it was his turn to hit, he wobbled to the tee, put the ball on the peg, and, with a furious swing, topped the ball with such force that it embedded in the ground six inches in front of the tee, popped out of its pitch mark, and rolled six feet backward. It was a hell of a shot; I mean, I couldn't have done that if I'd tried.

It was at once comical and sad. This man's mental state was the exact opposite of what it should have been. Instead of feeling calm and controlled, he was on the verge of panic. Rather than plan the type of shot he wanted to hit or focus on a swing key, it was all he could do to balance the ball on the tee. His thinking was so accelerated that in effect he wasn't thinking at all.

Golf has a way of doing that to you. Under pressure, especially when there are people watching, the inexperienced player tends to feel vulnerable, exposed, inept, and self-conscious. It is as though others can see right to your soul and see those feelings for themselves. It is a desperate sensation and one of the hardest for the rank amateur to overcome.

You must first recognize that the mental state necessary to function well in golf is different than for any other game. American football players find it helpful to scream, jump up and down, and bang each other on the head in order to get psyched up for the big game. Basketball coaches often work their players into a frenzied mental state just before tip-off. With golf, it is just the opposite. You don't want to get wildly pumped up, you want to slow down. You need to stabilize your thinking process so you can think clearly and rationally about the matter at hand.

When you are in the Zone, the pace of your thinking slows to the extent that things appear to happen in slow motion. When I was in Australia recently, I spent a week with race car driver Nigel Mansell. He told me that as he sped around the track at speeds up to 200 miles per hour, it felt more like 20 miles per hour. "When I go past the pits," he said, "I can see my wife clear as day. I can actually recognize friends."

How do you combat the nervousness that breeds a frantic mental state? I have five suggestions.

1. *Relish the opportunity to display your skill.* You wouldn't be reading this book if you didn't aspire to perform better in competitive situations, so when you get in one, remind yourself that this is the payoff for all of your hard work. Remember, too, that this is just one of many opportunities you'll have to succeed. It isn't a onetime, do-or-die thing.

2. *Ask yourself, what's the worst thing that can happen?* We all fear the unknown, and that is why it is difficult to be calm in a stressful situation. But when you think about it, the consequences of an embarrassing shot off the first tee aren't that severe. People will forget about it before you finish the first hole.

3. *Shut out everything around you.* This may sound difficult, but train your eyes only on the fairway or green, the ball, and your club. What you can't see can't hurt you.

4. *Take it one shot at a time.* Don't think about the consequences of a bogey or double bogey. The only shot that matters is the one you are playing. Getting ahead of yourself breeds too much excitement if things are going well, too much anxiety if they are going poorly.

5. *Work on your preshot routine.* Establishing a repetitive, rhythmic, systematic procedure of approaching the ball and hitting it establishes rhythm, trust, and confidence in your swing.

British race car driver Nigel Mansell, who is also an avid golfer, says that when he is performing well, he can recognize faces in the pit area even when whizzing by at 200 miles per hour.

By using these techniques, you will soon be amazed at how poised and calm you are regardless of the situation. You may feel the adrenaline pumping in some situations, but you will be able to control it.

Physical Relaxation

When you are mentally calm, you also are physically relaxed. This is very important, for when your muscles are relaxed and fluid, they move more quickly, have a greater range of motion, and tend to work in harmony with one another. Every good competitor knows this and learns how to keep his muscles loose, even under pressure.

Of course, this can be difficult when the adrenaline is flowing and you have butterflies, that knot that settles in the pit of your stomach when the heat is on. Amateurs don't get into pressure-inducing situations very often, and when they do, they are ill-equipped to handle it. In the case of my amateur playing partner in Missouri, the knot in his stomach quickly moved into every muscle in his body. By the time he addressed the ball, the veins in his arms were showing, his knuckles were white, and you could see the muscles in his neck. Clearly, his body was in no condition to do what his mind told it.

Experienced performers know how to look and feel physically relaxed even when their insides are churning. In fact, they welcome that knot in their stomach because it's a sign that they are alert and eager to perform. How do they do it? Experience is a big part of it. The more you play under pressure, the better your ability to stay loose and relaxed. Here are a few other hints.

1. *Stay in motion.* Muscle tension sets in easier when your limbs are still. Stretch your muscles. Walk about. Talk to someone. On the putting green, this isn't always practical. Tom Watson has a solution to this. Just before he putts, he shakes his hands out. This removes tension and enhances feel.

2. *Control your thinking.* Because physical tension begins in the mind, take charge of your thoughts and emotions. Put the keys to staying mentally calm to use.

3. *Employ the breath control training technique described in chapter 6.*

Low Anxiety

In the 1978 U.S. Open at Cherry Hills in Denver, Andy North came to the final hole needing a bogey 5 to win. After two decent shots, he faced a short pitch over a greenside bunker. North hit the shot poorly and it plopped into the sand. Now, if that doesn't breed anxiety, nothing will. But North, in full view of a huge gallery and national television audience, started laughing, obviously at himself for playing such a poor shot. He then waded into the bunker, took his time, and blasted out to within four feet of the cup. He made the putt and won his first of two U.S. Opens.

North's refusal to feel anxious and distraught over the poor shot was made possible because he was in the Zone. He was so firmly entrenched in the ideal performance state that a potentially catastrophic shot rolled off of him like water off a duck's back. He was not aware of the pressure because in his mental state, there was no pressure.

On the other hand, I have played in pro-ams with millionaires, proud and powerful men who every day make decisions that influence thousands of people, who turn to vanilla pudding on the golf course. Strong willed though they are, they are overcome by anxiety over their golf games. They rarely play to their handicap in competition because of their inability to lower their anxiety level.

Anxiety is destructive, and it doesn't take much to let it creep into your psyche. It may be caused by a bad shot or a poor decision. Sometimes the cause is more innocuous, like maybe worrying over a difficult hole still ahead or a tough opponent you will face in next week's club championship. In any case, the effects of anxiety are both psychological and physical. Mentally, anxiety leads to a negative attitude, nervousness, anger, and a lack of confidence. Physically, anxiety causes tension to pervade your body, stifling your ability to make a full, flowing swing. Your timing is disrupted and mistakes are sure to follow.

Andy North at the 1978 U.S. Open at Cherry Hills. A flubbed shot on the final hole didn't make Andy lose his composure.

On occasion, a certain amount of anxiety can be helpful. Being keyed up before an important round is natural and shows that you care about your golf game. It also is a sign of a healthy competitive spirit. The great Byron Nelson used to get so keyed up before tournaments that he sometimes became physically ill. Dr. Cary Middlecoff, who won two U.S. Opens and a Masters, found it almost impossible to sleep the night before an important round. When these fellows finally arrived at the first tee, however, their senses were so acute, their bodies so ready to perform, that they actually benefited by feeling anxious. Of course, these fellows had lots of experience at handling their performance anxiety.

Most of the time, anxiety is counterproductive. It can compound feelings of pressure and instill fear, worry, and trepidation. Here are some effective ways you can fight it.

1. *Improve your swing technique.* Anxiety often stems from the knowledge that your swing isn't sound. Devoting more time to practice, seeking sound swing instruction from your pro, and keeping yourself in good physical shape will improve your skill and strengthen your self-confidence.

2. *Watch your pace.* When you have a bad hole, it is extremely easy to become fast and careless. The same thing can happen if you have a streak of exceptionally good holes. No matter what happens, walk at the same speed and take the same amount of time on every shot. Not only does this conserve energy, it instills an element of flow into your round that leaves you less susceptible to feelings of anxiety.

3. *Increase your strength and stamina.* If you think back, you'll notice that anxiety usually creeps in toward the end of a round, not at the beginning. Most players attribute this to accumulating pressure, but more often it results from getting tired. When you tire physically, you are more prone to anxiety, lack of patience, and frustration. Eat wisely. Start an exercise program. When you play, drink plenty of fluids at regular intervals.

4. *Learn to relax between shots.* Dwelling on a bad shot, or worrying about a difficult one that lies ahead, is a chief cause of anxiety. You must learn to shift your attention to something else, if only for a minute. A moment's relaxation will help you maintain an optimistic, constructive attitude.

5. *Work on your preshot routine.* I made this point in chapter 2, but a preshot routine is also enormously effective at reducing anxiety. A good routine sets your body in motion, which in turn relaxes your muscles. It focuses your mind on executing the shot, not on the consequences of what missing the shot might mean.

Energy

The Zone consists of many elements, some of which seem contradictory at first glance. The qualities I've stressed so far— mental calmness, physical relaxation, and low anxiety—hardly seem compatible with energy as defined in the dictionary. Nevertheless, every top athlete is teeming with positive energy when he is in the ideal performance state. The question is, how can energy and calm coexist in the same psychological environment? And is it possible for them to interact in a positive way?

The answer is yes. Feeling energized does not mean your adrenaline is flowing so furiously that control over your physical actions is impaired. Nor is energy expressed only in physical terms. In the athletic sense, energized means feeling enraptured and exhilarated by the spirit of competition. It is a mixture of joy, enthusiasm, and love for golf and the opportunity to play your very best. It is largely psychological, although it manifests wonderfully in how well you perform physically.

In the 1977 British Open at Turnberry in Scotland, Tom Watson knocked in a three-foot birdie putt on the last hole to defeat Jack Nicklaus by one stroke. Paired together for the final two rounds, Jack and Tom waged an enormous battle that tested their mental toughness and playing skill. When it was over, Nicklaus stood up at the presentation ceremony and said, "I'm happy that Tom won. He played great and I gave it my best shot, but it just wasn't good enough. It was a great day of golf." Jack's

The 1977 British Open duel between Tom Watson and Jack Nicklaus gave us one of the most exciting moments in golf history. Though the contest was intense, both players acknowledged that fun and enjoyment were the overriding sensations.

comment made it clear that, in spite of an extremely disappointing setback, he was gratified to have the opportunity to test the depth of his talent.

Feeling energized invites other positive elements into the ideal performance state. When you are charged with enthusiasm, you also feel more optimistic, bright, and alert. You are more resilient to bad breaks, poor weather, and lousy course conditions. Physically, your strength and stamina increase.

Not all energy has positive effects. There are four types of energy and it is vital that you utilize the right kind. Let's define them.

1. *High-positive energy.* This is the type of energy climate you want to obtain. Mentally, you are alert, determined, aggressive, lively, stimulated, vigorous, and enthused. Physically, your muscles are relaxed yet highly responsive to commands from your brain. You have the best chance of succeeding when you have this type of energy working for you. This is the state Jack Nicklaus and Tom Watson were in at Turnberry.

2. *High-negative energy.* In this state, you are too pumped up physically and your mental state is characterized by nervousness and high anxiety. This is acceptable in some sports, such as football, but it has no place in golf. This is because the game demands precise control over your smaller muscles, and feeling agitated or overly excited impairs control over hands and arms.

A golfer who leads a tournament overnight is prone to high-negative energy when he starts out in the final round the next day. The U.S. Open has often had relative unknowns lead after the first round, but the worry and fear generated by their unexpected success usually leads to this state and hinders their ability to sustain a good performance. It is possible to play well with high-negative energy if your technique is sound and you manage to settle down. More often than not, however, you'll play worse than expected.

3. *Low-positive energy.* Here you feel positive and calm, but physically you are "dead." You see a lot of this at the U.S. Am-

ateur Championship. Players are required to play two qualifying rounds and then two eighteen-hole matches per day the first two days of the tournament proper. Toward the end of the week, some of the players simply run out of gas. Few amateurs are conditioned to so strenuous a schedule. The resulting fatigue slows reflexes, saps your strength, and depletes psychological energy. It is possible to play well in this condition—Ken Venturi won the 1964 U.S. Open in a state of near physical collapse—but most of the time you will fail.

4. *Low-negative energy.* This player has no chance. Mentally you feel bored and get annoyed easily. Physically your muscles are lax and unresponsive. You don't see this type of mental state on the PGA Tour, because you can't perform at a high level when you feel this way. But it's common on the amateur level. Ever play with someone who moans that he "just doesn't have it today" and carries a hangdog expression on his face? That's low-negative energy.

To further identify high-positive energy, let's look at two situations where a golfer is in that mode. The following thought processes are typical.

Situation A

"I shot my worst round of the year at this course last year, but there's no way I'm going to play poorly here again. I've worked on the type of shots the layout demands. I have my course strategy mapped out. I'm well rested and have taken care of everything at work so I can focus on this round. I won't be denied!"

Situation B

"This guy beat me in the club championship last year, and I know he thinks he'll have an easy time with me again. Boy, is he in for a surprise. I'm going to hang tough in this match like it's the last one I'll ever play. I'm going to put pressure on him right out of the box, and this time we'll see how he handles it.

I'm going to enjoy shaking his hand when it's over and saying, 'Nice match, better luck next time.'"

Your own thought processes in the high-positive energy mode may vary, but the basic characteristics are the same for everyone. To attain this state, you must learn to eliminate the negativism that golf by its nature imparts on all of us. If your bad play in competition is due to a poor attitude, monitor your thinking. The second you hear yourself saying something like, "I hate this hole," "That lucky guy gets so many breaks it's unreal," or "That's the worst pin location I've ever seen on a green," STOP. Replace the negative thought with something more positive. Force-feed positive thoughts to yourself, even if they seem contrived or faked. A few positive thoughts and feelings will set up a chain reaction of constructive thoughts and will lead to the high-positive state.

Optimism

Of the five PGA championships Walter Hagen won in the 1920s, his last, captured in Dallas in 1927, was perhaps the most compelling. Against Joe Turnesa in the championship match, Hagen was one down with two holes to play. Turnesa drove safely on the seventeenth and Hagen followed with a wild drive into knee-high rough. As he walked to his ball, Hagen laughed and joked, telling his followers that he would probably find his ball teed up in a nice spot.

When Hagen got to his ball, it was indeed sitting in a beautiful patch of mown grass cut by the fairway mower as it traveled from one fairway over to another. It was unbelievable luck and Hagen took advantage of it, knocking his approach shot three feet from the hole. Hagen squared the match, and then won on the first extra hole.

That was Hagen—confident, optimistic, sure that things would somehow go his way. Most of the time, things did. Hagen never got upset over a poor shot. He knew he was likely to hit several poor shots during a round and didn't overreact when he did. By maintaining an optimistic frame of mind, he stayed calm,

Walter Hagen, winner of five PGA Championships, was an eternal optimist. He expected good breaks—and usually got them.

relaxed, and in complete control of his golf game. And, for some unexplained reason, good things seemed to happen to him.

Obviously, optimism is much more constructive than pessimism. But some people are more optimistic by nature than others and don't have to confront this problem very often. Chip Beck is one of the most cheerful and effervescent people I know off the golf course, and it seems to rub off on his demeanor during competition. He is always upbeat, energetic, and aware. Al Geiberger is the same way. Other golfers (like me, for example) are forced to pay more attention to this element of mental toughness. This can be difficult, especially in golf where the amateur is almost certain to hit as many bad shots as good ones during the course of a round.

So how can you be optimistic when your last three putts for par have lipped the cup and come to rest on the edge of the hole? There are two ways of thinking of this. You can look at it and say, "I guess it's one of those days when nothing is going in," or you can say, "I'm putting pretty well if I'm hitting the hole every time. It's only a matter of time before they start dropping."

Optimism also can be triggered by bringing to mind certain thoughts and images. I've found that on a day when I'm grumpy and pessimistic, thinking of something humorous brightens my mood and attitude considerably. Whistling a cheerful tune in my mind can accomplish the same thing. The most effective way to become optimistic is through action, like holing a long putt or hitting a spectacular sand shot. If you are so fatally pessimistic that you don't give yourself a chance to hit a mood-elevating shot, you're shooting yourself in the foot.

Enjoyment

Golf is meant to be fun, yet there are many fine players, amateur and professional, who have quit playing altogether because they don't enjoy it anymore. A friend of mine, who shall remain nameless, was at one time an excellent player. But after he left the pro tour, he hardly ever picked up a club. "It's no fun any-

more," he told me. "I can't play as well as I used to and I get disgusted shooting high scores. It's better not to play at all."

At the other end of the spectrum are golfers like the late Glenna Collett Vare, who won six U.S. Women's Amateur championships in the 1920s and continued playing golf almost up until the time she died in 1989. Ben Hogan retired from competitive golf eighteen years ago, yet he still loves to go out to his club, Shady Oaks in Fort Worth, and hit practice balls.

In any walk of life, you perform better when you enjoy what you're doing, and golf is no exception. When you are enthused and stimulated by the game, you play better. What causes enjoyment to decrease for some golfers? The object in golf is to shoot the lowest score possible, and accomplishing that requires intelligent thought and physical effort. When you hit bad shots, the natural reaction is disgust and displeasure. How do you manage those days when nothing seems to go right? How can you make the game more enjoyable regardless of your performance?

Here are my solutions.

1. *Be frank about your ability.* If you are a bonafide thirteen-handicapper, don't get bent out of shape if you play to a 15. Your range of scores is likely to vary and you have to accept it. If you find it difficult to be satisfied with so-so rounds, work on your game so you'll improve. But in the meantime, smell the flowers. Enjoy the companionship and what good shots you hit. I strongly urge you to practice, for you're sure to receive two distinct types of pleasures: the pride and satisfaction that comes through improving and the sheer fun of being able to play at a level you weren't capable of before.

2. *Ask yourself, why am I out here?* If you play golf merely to shoot a good score, you had better temper that with the qualification that you have fun as well. Even in competition, remember that golf is a game and the essential reason for playing is for recreation and enjoyment.

3. *Lower your expectation level.* You'll be surprised at how much more relaxed and adept you'll be if you don't live and die

Glenna Collett Vare was a tough and serious competitor, yet she never lost sight of the fact that golf is a game to be enjoyed.

with every stroke you make. Play the game as well as you are capable of playing. You can't ask for more. As you improve your skill, your expectation level naturally will rise. But don't ask more than you're capable of producing.

4. *Seek out enjoyable playing companions.* The reason many golfers play with their regular foursome every weekend is that they enjoy each other's company. Even tour pros like to play practice rounds with their friends. If you play with miserable people, you'll eventually adopt their attitude. If you play with golfers you are comfortable with, it will be much easier to make the occasional transition to playing with serious, intense competitors.

5. *Make your games interesting.* Think up unusual bets. Switch playing partners. Play the back nine first. The more stimulating you make the game, the more fun you'll have. This applies to practice as well. The more innovative and unusual you make your practice, the less boring and more productive it becomes.

Effortless

The eighteenth hole at Augusta National Golf Club, site of the Masters Tournament, is one of the great finishing holes in golf. The hole doglegs to the right, and about 260 yards from the teeing ground is a fairway bunker. At the 1988 Masters, Sandy Lyle came to this hole tied for the lead. To eliminate the possibility of driving his tee shot into the bunker, Lyle chose a 1-iron. He then hit that 1-iron into the sand. He couldn't believe he hit the ball that far with an iron, and neither could the television announcers. Lyle hit a spectacular sand shot and birdied the hole to win, but to this day people are still raving about how Sandy drove the ball 260 yards with a 1-iron. He made it look so easy. That's what happens when you are in the Zone. You hit the ball farther with less effort, putt better with less conscious thought, and control your emotions with ease.

You no doubt have had days where success has come with less effort. The challenge is to adopt this trait and then sustain

When Sandy Lyle won the 1988 Masters, he made difficult shots look easy.

it. Very often, golfers get into the Zone early in a round, then wake up when they realize what they are doing. I can't tell you how many times I've seen players display beautiful rhythm for sixteen holes, only to become choppy and forced when they realize they have a chance to shoot a good score. Not only do they alter their swing, they change their strategy.

Most often, they start trying too hard. This prompts a change in the type of energy they have. They go from high-positive to high-negative and experience increased muscle tension and mental intensity. They involuntarily discard the one element that got them there to begin with. They leave the Zone and find it almost impossible to get back into it.

"Letting it happen" is one of the biggest challenges in golf and is a key aspect of the Zone. You cannot force an effortless quality into the constellation of mental skills. It's like driving a car. As you drive down the road, you press on the gas pedal and brake instinctively. Your hands make tiny little corrective movements on the steering wheel. You shift gears. You do all of this while having a conversation and listening to the radio. But what would happen if, as you pulled out of a parking lot, you told yourself, "Okay, turn the wheel exactly ninety degrees to the right. Hold the wheel for one second, then turn the other way forty degrees. Press the gas pedal down three inches until the car reaches forty miles per hour. Check the rearview mirror every three seconds exactly."

Obviously, if you tried to drive a car in this manner you'd get in a wreck within five seconds. You have to operate the car by responding to the visual and audible activity around you. You don't actively think about it.

The effortless mode in golf is much the same way. When you are in the Zone, you merely respond to data entering the sensory part of your brain. You see the part of the fairway you want to hit your ball to, get in position at address, and fire away.

Here's a drill to demonstrate how effortlessly your body can function when it merely reacts to images from the mind. The next time you practice putting, station yourself thirty feet from the hole and stand away from the ball. Make practice strokes

while looking at the hole, gauging the amount of backswing necessary to make the ball go at the target. Now address the ball and hit the putt while looking at the hole. You'll be surprised at how accurately your mind assesses the speed of the putt and how effortlessly it transmits this information to your hands and arms. This is the way you want to play golf—merely reacting to elements in your environment.

Automatic

In the Watson-Nicklaus duel at Turnberry in 1977, I could scarcely believe the way Watson played the last hole. After splitting the fairway with his tee shot, he had an all-important 7-iron shot to the green. When it was time to hit, he pulled that club from the bag, addressed the ball, and hit it so quickly that the television cameras almost missed it. From the pace of his preshot routine and the swing itself, you couldn't distinguish that shot from any other he hit during the round. It embodied the word automatic.

How often I see golfers perform just the opposite of Watson! It's called "paralysis by analysis" and it is one of the great destroyers of timing, rhythm, and overall performance. Usually it occurs early in the round, when golfers are a little anxious as to "how the ball is flying" that day, or late in the round, when they feel each stroke is more critical than the last. They think that taking a little more time, studying the shot more carefully, and checking your grip and setup more precisely will help ensure a good shot. Actually, just the opposite occurs.

It all goes back to the nature of the game I discussed in chapter 2. Golf is played from a static start, and it is important to establish inner rhythm and remain faithful to that rhythm at all times. If you alter that rhythm, you are sure to destroy the inner flow that helps you swing smoothly and decisively.

The cure for this, like so many parts of the Zone, is to work on your preshot routine and use it on every stroke, regardless of the situation. Pressure doesn't change the demands of playing a shot, so why change your approach to hitting it?

Alertness

Jack Nicklaus has won twenty major championships, but the one he says was most gratifying was his fourth U.S. Open title at Baltusrol in New Jersey in 1980. Willie Anderson, Ben Hogan, and Bobby Jones were the only players in history to have won four Opens, and Jack wanted this one badly. On the final hole he sank a birdie putt for the title and the crowd went absolutely wild. They poured onto the green to congratulate him. Jack's caddie, Angelo Argea, ran up to Jack, ready to sweep him in his arms.

But wait. Jack stood back, spread his arms, and said, "Hold it." Jack's playing partner, Isao Aoki of Japan, hadn't holed out yet. Before Jack allowed the celebration to begin, he allowed U.S. Golf Association officials to clear the green so Aoki could finish.

Not only was this a terrific act of sportsmanship, it indicated how alert Jack was. He had just won the most important title to that point in his career, and he had the presence of mind to notice that Aoki hadn't finished putting.

Nicklaus did a similar thing at the 1969 Ryder Cup matches. Jack was playing against England's Tony Jacklin, the reigning British Open champion. The team score was tied as they played the final hole. Nicklaus sank a very difficult eight-foot putt for par. Now it was up to Jacklin to make a three-foot putt to halve the match and even the overall score. Nicklaus walked over and picked up Tony's ball, in effect conceding the putt. Jack later said, "There is no better way for these matches to finish than all square." Some of the Americans were upset that Jack didn't make Tony putt, but that isn't the point here. Jack's knowledge of where the match stood and the importance of his putt and Jacklin's was a fabulous demonstration of total awareness and alertness.

Alertness is a crucial element of the Zone. Billy Casper, who won the 1959 and 1966 U.S. Opens as well as the 1970 Masters, once said that when he walked down the fairway, he always kept his head up. "It's like the jungle," Casper said. "Those with their heads down get eaten." Casper is referring to the impor-

Billy Casper, a keen competitor who is always alert to events going on around him.

tance of staying acutely aware of everything going on about you. When you are alert, you receive all types of useful information that figures into the process of hitting golf shots, such as the firmness of greens or the direction of the wind.

To improve your alertness, try this exercise. When you arrive home after a round, sit in your favorite chair, close your eyes, and see if you can reconstruct the round down to the tiniest detail. Try to remember not only every shot but the type of lie you had, which way the wind was blowing, and how many times your ball bounced on the green before rolling to a stop. You may not do very well at first. The next time you play, resolve before the round to commit all of these details to memory. This will force you to be more alert and aware.

Self-Confidence

I always laugh when the third-round leader of a major championship tells the press, "Tomorrow is just another round of golf for me. I'm going to treat it like any other." It's a sure sign of wavering self-confidence. Here they are on the threshold of winning the most important title of their lives, and they're saying it's just another tournament. What they're really doing is leaving themselves with an out, a safety valve, in case they don't play well enough to win the next day.

Self-confidence is perhaps the most important quality a champion can have. A strong I-can-do-it attitude atones for many weaknesses. Self-confidence helps you maintain your calm and poise so that under pressure, your perspective of the situation is much more sober and realistic. Greg Norman is filled with self-confidence; it's what enables him to play the bold style of golf he does. Lanny Wadkins also is self-confident; he never gets intimidated and has an unwavering belief in his ability to hit every shot close to the hole.

Unlike other elements of the Zone, self-confidence can't be manufactured. It is something you develop through positive experiences. That is why practice is so important. When you face a difficult shot late in the round, you have to know you can pull it off. A little self-doubt will kill you in that situation.

No golfer is more self-confident than Lanny Wadkins.

As bold as some self-confident golfers seem by the way they talk and perform, it nevertheless is a delicate thing that can be destroyed by a bad experience. I am amazed at how Greg Norman has kept his self-confidence intact after losing two major championships on extremely fortunate shots by Larry Mize and Bob Tway. There are few better examples of mental toughness and resiliency.

Smart players know how delicate genuine self-confidence is, and they do everything possible to keep it intact. As bold a player as Norman is, you'll rarely see him attempt a shot he has little chance of bringing off successfully. If he were to hit it poorly, it would shatter his self-confidence because of the humiliation he would feel at making a dumb decision. Tom Kite and Mike Reid are the same way. They only play shots they know they can play well, and gamble only when they have to.

In Control

I was paired with Gary Player in the Australian Open one year during the mid-1970s. He was in an excellent position to win. Gary is from South Africa, and to that point in time his government had showed no signs of relaxing its controversial apartheid policy. On this occasion, Gary's presence in the field prompted many public demonstrations against Player and his country.

During the tournament, Gary received a death threat. He decided to play anyway, and it was an experience I'll never forget. Vandals had snuck out on the course the previous night and whitewashed six greens with the words, "Pig Go Home." I knew darn well Gary was affected by such a vicious personal attack, yet he played on doggedly and won the tournament. I was impressed by his enormous self-control. An incident like that could have sparked many emotions—fear, anger, resentment, self-pity—but Gary kept all of those negative feelings under wraps.

Being in control means you are in charge of events rather than letting events take charge over you. There are so many things in golf you have no control over—bad breaks, the elements, playing partners who chatter ceaselessly—but while you

Bobby Jones had a fiery temper as a boy, but he later learned to control it.

can't control them, you can control the way they affect you. In the 1977 U.S. Open at Southern Hills, Hubert Green played the last round in the company of U.S. Marshals. The reason: a death threat that had been phoned in before Hubert teed off. Green was a portrait of poise that last day, winning the tournament under extraordinarily difficult conditions. Hubert simply ignored the death threat and concentrated on his golf. He had enough self-control and mental discipline to play extremely well.

Control is largely a matter of maturity. The young Bobby Jones had an awful temper, often throwing clubs and sulking when he wasn't playing well. In the 1921 British Open at St. Andrews, Jones became so upset he tore up his scorecard and walked off the course. Jones was so ashamed of the incident that he swore never to lose his temper on the golf course again. And he didn't. Even today, many young touring pros tend to get upset over little things, such as camera shutters clicking, or someone in the gallery yelling as they stand over a putt. Heaven knows things like that used to drive me crazy. Through time, however, you learn that these things come with the territory and you learn to forget them quickly.

At this time, look back at chapter 3 and the heading, "In control of their emotions." More information on being in control is included there.

Summary

In this chapter we have listed the eleven elements of the Zone and outlined some strategies for acquiring them. In chapter 5, we will discuss techniques that will improve your performance in each area and help you utilize them all at once.

A great deal of information has been presented to this point, and I understand how difficult it is to commit all of it to memory. However, the nature of this training program requires that you comprehend one facet before moving on to the next. For this reason, I suggest you review this chapter before turning the page. And don't leave it at that. As you read chapter 5, take time on occasion to return to this chapter. It will clarify the relationship between your goal—the Zone—and the techniques for acquiring it.

5

Putting the Package Together

Techniques That Work

From the time I joined the PGA Tour in 1971, I have heard numerous locker room debates on the topic, "What Makes Jack Nicklaus Great?" It's a popular subject, and I am always amused by the disagreement that arises when Jack's fellow pros try to identify the single aspect of his game that enabled him to play better than anybody else for almost twenty-five years.

Relatively few players cite Jack's outstanding physical ability as the primary reason for his success. His talent and technical skill are immense, but over the years the PGA Tour has had better ball strikers than Nicklaus. There also have been better putters, sand players, and short game experts. No, the pros usually cite some aspect of Jack's superior mental approach to the game. That is the part of his game they covet most and have been unable to emulate. In tournament play, Nicklaus displays an intangible quality that confounds, intimidates, and pressures other pros. It is a mixture of confidence, poise, toughness, exuberance, determination, enthusiasm, and concentration. Put together, they produce an aura of invincibility.

In trying to isolate the strongest aspect of Jack's mental approach, someone will say, "Jack's secret is his confidence. He has more faith in his ability to execute under pressure than anyone in history." Someone will respond, "I say it's his concentration. He is totally focused on his game when the heat is on and nothing can distract him." Others mention his composure, his pride, his imagination.

When Jack Nicklaus adopts "the Look," other golfers are filled with a sense of awe.

All of these opinions are accurate, but they miss the point. It is not Jack's outstanding excellence in a single area that makes him a superior golfer. Rather, it is his ability to harness together many psychological and emotional components and utilize them simultaneously that sets him apart from others. Nicklaus and a few others, such as Seve Ballesteros, Greg Norman, and Tom Watson, have learned to achieve a state of mind where many positive attributes are working for them at the same time. That is what the Zone is all about. When a number of powerful components come together at the same time, incredible feats are possible.

In describing the sensation of being in the Zone, I've used adjectives like "mystical" and "magical." That is entirely accurate, but I don't want to leave the impression that getting there requires chanting phrases from a sorcerer's handbook. On the contrary, it can be obtained by using simple, straightforward techniques that have existed in one form or another for years. In fact, you probably have used these techniques to some degree yourself.

As my study of the Zone progressed after I won the U.S. Open, I discovered that my periods of inconsistency and poor play could immediately be traced to poor utilization of these techniques. I found, to my surprise and satisfaction, that increasing my effort in one or two areas improved the frequency with which I entered the ideal performance state. Today, I have no doubt about the correlation between these techniques and the heightened performance that occurs when you are in the Zone.

Although the task of pulling together all of the elements of the Zone seems formidable, it really is not. Sure, some of the following techniques require some effort and persistence. But you will be profoundly pleased with the results they produce.

Visualization: Seeing is Doing

The 1982 U.S. Open at Pebble Beach Golf Links was the most important tournament of Tom Watson's life. At age thirty-three, he already had won two British Opens and two Masters

tournaments. Now came the title he wanted more than any other. Watson played brilliantly the first three rounds and came to the seventeenth hole the final day tied with Jack Nicklaus, who had already finished his round.

The seventeenth at Pebble is a difficult par 3 requiring a long-iron shot to an elusive green. Watson went through his preshot routine smoothly, got set, then hit his 2-iron shot into tall rough just left of the green. This was not the place to be. From there, he faced a delicate little chip to a fast green sloping away from him. A par, which he needed badly, seemed unlikely.

As Tom completed sizing up the shot, his caddie, Bruce Edwards, told him quietly, "Get it close." Watson's reply has since become famous. "I'm not going to get it close," he said, "I'm going to make it." Unbelievably, Watson holed the chip shot and then birdied the par-5 eighteenth to win by two strokes.

In a sense, Watson holed the chip shot before he hit it. He "saw" the ball going into the hole as he stood over the ball at address. It was all programmed in advance—the type of stroke he would make, the arc of the ball as it popped off the club face, the soft bounce on the edge of the green, the smooth roll into the cup. There is no better example of visualization.

The body's ability to perform precise movements based on a general picture from the mind is extraordinary. During World War II, American soldiers in training were encouraged to imagine themselves performing in combat, so the experience wouldn't be so jarring when it actually occurred. Actors have always visualized themselves "becoming" the character they are about to play. When you apply for a job or ask your boss for a raise, you no doubt picture the situation in advance to better anticipate questions and answers.

Visualization has always had a prominent place in golf. When Larry Mize holed a difficult six-foot putt to get into a play-off for the 1987 Masters, he said it was made easier by a game he used to play by himself as a youngster. Mize said he used to conclude his practice putting by standing over a ten-footer and saying, "This is for the Masters." Seve Ballesteros is credited with being the most imaginative golfer in the world for his ability

Tom Watson holing the famous chip shot to defeat Jack Nicklaus in the 1982 U.S. Open at Pebble Beach. Watson "saw" the ball going in the hole even before he hit it.

Seve Ballesteros is a remarkable trouble shot player, mostly because he can visualize the unusual swings necessary to play them.

to think up unusual shots from trouble around the greens. Seve visualizes the type of swing he wants to make before he hits the shot.

Some golfers seem to be blessed with strong visualization skills, while others aren't. When I'm visualizing well, I see things happening in great detail. I see the path the clubhead will follow on the backswing and downswing. I can hear the "crack" of the clubface meeting the ball. I see the divot flying in the air, the ball zipping to the target. This certainly has been true with me during my best performances.

Some golfers seem to be blessed with strong visualization skills, while others aren't. But the great thing about visualization is, you can improve it regardless of how well you can visualize things at present. It is a learned skill, and developing it is important if you are to get the most out of your ideal performance state. The following exercise will help you evaluate and improve your visualization skill.

Close your eyes and imagine yourself playing a standard 5-iron shot to a green where the flagstick is located on the back right portion of the green. Imagine it in as much detail as possible. Now see if you can answer these questions about the experience.

1. What was your lie like? Was the ball sitting up, or was it nestled down in the grass?

2. Did you hit the ball solidly, fat, or thin? How did the sensation of the clubhead striking the ball register in your hands? How did it feel?

3. What did the shot sound like? Did it make a distinct "thwock" noise, or an unsatisfying "whumph?"

4. What was the trajectory of the ball? Did it hook or slice?

5. How many times did the ball bounce before it began rolling?

6. Did you take a divot? How large was it?

7. Did the experience happen in color or black and white?

What color were your shoes, pants, and shirt? Were you wearing a hat?

If you can answer these questions accurately, your powers of visualization and recall are pretty good already. If you can't remember many details, you can improve by doing this exercise every day. In addition, there are other techniques that will not only help you form a clear mental picture of your swing but help you actuate the scene you are imagining. Those techniques, described below, should be performed in a quiet, nondistracting environment, at a time when your mind is free and clear. The more often you do them, the more effective they become.

- *Take a video of your swing and study it closely.* When Billy Casper, a two-time U.S. Open champion and winner of the 1970 Masters, was mired in a deep slump in 1982, he sought the help of sports psychologist Cliff Webb of Provo, Utah. One thing Webb did was compile film footage of Casper achieving his most memorable triumphs. Billy watched them over and over, ingraining those visual and emotional images into his mind. Billy acknowledges that this helped him tremendously, and he has gone on to be a very successful player on the Senior PGA Tour.

  The same tactic can work for you. Get to know how your swing looks and marry the visual information into how your swing feels. You can do the same thing swinging a club in front of a full-length mirror or examining still photographs of your swing.

- *What's the most difficult shot for you to hit?* Picture yourself bringing this shot off successfully. Repeat it over and over, at least ten times until you can't see yourself failing.

- *Imagine that you've just hit your ball in the water.* Call to mind your typical feeling of anger and frustration. Now start over and picture yourself hitting the ball in the water again. This time, although you feel peeved, you recover your emotional control immediately and approach the drop area reso-

Billy Casper watched films of his winning the 1966 U.S. Open to in-grain positive images in his mind.

lutely and with poise. You don't smile, but neither do you frown. Your attention shifts to playing the next shot.

As your ability to create vivid mental pictures increases, your next goal is to translate those visual images into physical action. This can be difficult, for it not only requires a sharp picture of what you want to accomplish but sufficient physical skill for you to perform what your mind sees. If, for instance, you visualize a 280-yard drive with a 5-yard curve from left to right, there is no possible way your body can perform what your mind sees. The extra effort you demand of your body will only result in a poor shot, disappointment, and anxiety. Your mental images always need to be realistic, and in the beginning they also should be simple.

Go out to your practice putting green with one ball and your putter. Preferably, you should pick a time when not many other golfers are around. Drop the ball six feet from a hole. Look at the putt from all angles, so you are sure of the break. Now gauge the speed of the green. Next, make a few practice strokes, quietly sensing how hard you need to hit the ball for it to trickle to the front edge of the hole and fall in. Imagine the feel of the ball impacting the sweet spot on the putter face. Picture the ball rolling end over end toward the hole and dropping in. Think of the sound the ball will make as it rattles into the cup. Keeping your body relaxed and your mind quiet, go ahead and strike the putt. Don't be discouraged if you miss it. Hit the same putt again and see if you can narrow the gap between what your mind sees and what your body actually does.

As is the case when you are actually playing a round, you should be devoid of mechanical thoughts. If you are preoccupied with technical aspects of the stroke, you will impede the flow of sensory images to your muscles. It all goes back to my U.S. Open experience, where I was on "automatic pilot." When you are playing well, your body is simply responding to those terrific images from your mind.

Negative Visualization

How often have you stood on the tee of a hole with water on the right, told yourself you must avoid that water at all costs,

Bruce Edwards, who caddied for Tom Watson for sixteen years, has a knack for instilling positive thinking in his employer.

and then promptly hit the ball into the water? Few things make a golfer more angry with himself. But it happens simply because, whether you wanted to or not, you visualized it happening.

A key to visualizing properly is to picture only positive events. When you assess the type of shot you want to hit, you certainly want to take into consideration hazards, out-of-bounds, bunkers, etc. But before you begin the backswing, it is imperative that your last visual thought be a positive one, because that is the one you are likely to execute.

Have you ever carried a song around in your head for an entire morning? With most people, that song is most likely to be the last one they heard on their car radio before they turned the car off. Visualization is much the same way. Make your last thought a positive one.

Watson's caddie, Bruce Edwards, caddied for me once at the 1985 Dunhill Cup, won by my native Australia. I had not been

playing well prior to the event. On the practice tee, Bruce told me, "David, you really are swinging very well. Your rhythm is fantastic." Whether this was true or not, it helped me visualize smooth rhythm and tempo, and I played very well.

Bruce told me another thing that has always stuck with me. "Byron Nelson told Tom one day that during his prime, the last shot he hit on the practice range was a perfect 1-iron," Bruce said. "Byron told Tom that this enabled him to go to the first tee with a very pleasing visual image." I've taken to doing this and it has done wonders for my confidence and my ability to visualize a good shot on the first tee. Of course, you may not be able to hit a perfect 1-iron shot if you stood on the practice range all day, so you may want to hit a perfect 7-iron shot instead.

Breathing and Relaxation

Early in his career, Tom Watson was blessed with tremendous physical and technical golfing skills, not to mention a good imagination. But after winning his first Masters title in 1977, he said, "When I learned how to breathe, I learned how to win."

What Watson meant was, for some time he had difficulty coping with the stress and strain of big-time tournament pressure. He performed well but struggled with his emotions more than he felt was necessary. Tom is fairly high-strung anyway, and he needed some way to relax sufficiently so he could control his thoughts and actions.

Tom found a solution in the unlikely area of controlling his breathing. When you are under pressure and stress, a number of physiological events occur that are difficult to control. Adrenaline pours into your system, giving you increased strength and energy. Coagulants are injected into your bloodstream, a phenomenon that in primitive times was meant to stifle bleeding when humans were confronted by a predator. Your capillaries recede farther below your skin, giving you a whiter, pale appearance. Your heart rate increases. Your mouth becomes dry. Your pupils become smaller, reducing your field of vision.

Finally, your breathing becomes more rapid and shallow.

This is to ensure that sufficient oxygen is distributed to your heart and other organs. When all of these things happen, it becomes difficult to control your smaller muscles. They may move more quickly than you want and may not give you the delicate feedback you need. You also tend to think more rapidly and may feel confused, fearful, and out of control.

All of this is natural as part of the fight-or-flight response God gave all animals. The phenomenon may have once been useful when man had to fight off animals in the jungle, but there is no place for it in golf. It is extremely difficult to ward off these effects, for they occur involuntarily. But you can decrease the flow of adrenaline into your system, slow your heart rate, and feel more in control of your physical actions by governing your breathing. By consciously slowing your breathing rate, you in turn slow your heart rate and decrease the flow of adrenaline into your system. You will feel more relaxed and able to function.

How often have you heard the expression, "take a deep breath" in athletics? Baseball pitchers take a deep, noticeable breath before throwing the crucial pitch on a 3-2 count. Basketball players take a deep breath before they attempt a crucial free throw. Tennis players learn to exhale sharply, or "grunt," at the moment they make a stroke. And in golf, you'll very often see players take a deep breath before hitting an important shot or attempting a nerve-wracking putt. Whether it's done consciously or unconsciously, there is a purpose for it. When you are in the Zone, it is imperative that you maintain the delicate physical and emotional balance that allows you to play your best.

Study the following deep-breathing technique. If you haven't tried it before, you may be surprised at how it relaxes you. Then I will explain how you can perform a variation of it on the golf course.

Step 1: Find a dark, quiet room and sit in a comfortable chair.

Take several deep breaths through your nostrils, holding
r one or two seconds before exhaling slowly. Let the

steady flow of air fill and expand the central part of your body. Think of something quiet and pleasant, such as a mountain stream or a breeze blowing gently through a stand of trees.

Step 3: When you exhale, also do so through your nose, so the air is released slowly and continuously. As you release the air, imagine letting tension release from the muscles in your arms, neck, torso, and legs. Try to feel as loose and limp as a rag doll.

Step 4: Perform this exercise for at least five minutes, longer if you can. When you are finished, rise slowly from the chair, exit the room, and go about your normal activities a little more slowly and drowsily.

The purpose is to dramatize the relaxing effect of breathing. Once you appreciate how profoundly it affects your tension level, you will be encouraged to use a variation of it on the golf course. For that purpose, I recommend the following.

- Before you tee off on the first hole, stand aside for a moment and take a few deep, slow breaths. Again, try to feel the tension seeping out of your body. Make some long, slow practice swings, keying on a relaxing thought such as "smooth."

- When you hit a bad shot, call a personal time-out and take one or two deep breaths. Walk slowly to your ball, relaxed but intent about following up with a good shot.

- When you face a critical putt, take one long, slow, deep breath before approaching the ball. Again, feel the tension flowing out of your hands and arms.

- In all situations, monitor your breathing patterns. If you find you are breathing more quickly than is normal, STOP. Stand still for a few moments and take slow, deep breaths until your breathing rate returns to normal.

Controlling your breathing is usually done to calm yourself down, but it also can be altered so as to help pump you up when

you are feeling listless and uninspired. Taking a few short, "huffy" breaths will immediately enliven your body and spirit, so you are more alert and attentive.

The Importance of Role Models

Modeling yourself after a personal hero is natural even for adults and is extremely useful. Human beings are great imitators, and we are conditioned to behave like those we admire and are exposed to most. In golf, copying someone whose style, presence, and technique you respect will speed your development. This was especially true with me, both as a youngster and as a professional.

My first hero was George Naismith, the professional at Riversdale, the course where I had my first job in golf. Mr. Naismith was a respected player and an excellent teacher, and I respected him a great deal. Although I played left-handed, I switched to playing right-handed the first time he suggested it. It was a change I was later glad to have made. He helped me build a foundation for my game.

Then I copied Alex Mercer, an Australian pro who, though a shaky putter, had a beautiful, flowing swing. I copied his grip and swing tempo. Later, I tried to copy Gary Player, the first world-class golfer I saw play. I didn't copy Gary's swing, but I certainly tried to adopt his dedication, determination, and tenacity. By incorporating Gary's persistence, enthusiasm, and constant search for knowledge into my game, I was able to hang in there when other golfers might have quit.

Later still, I copied Bruce Devlin. Bruce was a real gentleman and had a fine, even temperament on the course. He was well liked by people off the course. I wanted to be more like that, and whether Bruce knew it or not, I began to adopt aspects of his personality.

My other big role model was Jack Nicklaus. The thing I admired most about Jack was his on-course demeanor, his total absorption into the game. By emulating his exemplary emotional control and intensity, I became less prone to the wild emotional swings that cost me dearly early in my career. I picked up on

*Bruce Devlin became one of my role models for his beautiful swing
tempo and his impeccable behavior off the golf course.*

parts of Jack's golf technique, too, such as choosing an inter-mediate target at address and precise alignment.

So, as you can see, I didn't have one role model but several. As an impressionable young man, I copied technique, attitude, dress, and behavior. Today, I guess I'm a composite of several good golfers. But, by incorporating favorable characteristics of each, I've emerged with my own style. It is very flattering when a youngster approaches me, asks for my autograph, and tells me he wants to be like me.

In choosing your role model, I suggest you select someone who is of the same height and build as you. If you're five feet, nine inches, you probably shouldn't try to copy the upright swing of, say, Nick Faldo, who is six feet, three inches. Some-one of more average height, like Larry Nelson or Tom Kite, would make more sense.

Make sure that the techniques you copy are sound. Some-thing that may look good aesthetically, such as a loop at the top of the backswing, may not be sound for you. Check with a professional on these matters.

Superstition

My feeling about golf is, if it works, use it. There is nothing about superstition that has a direct physical effect on your ability to perform well, yet it seems to provide a source of familiarity and comfort for some golfers, a feeling that they have something extra going for them. Even well-known professionals have su-perstitions. For instance:

- Sandy Lyle won the 1988 Masters wearing a tan shirt and plaid pants. The next week, at the MCI Heritage Classic in South Carolina, Lyle showed up wearing the same clothes—washed, of course.

- Charles Coody, the 1971 Masters champion, always marked his ball with an old coin minted in the 1800s.

- Jack Nicklaus used to always put his left golf shoe on first, and he insisted on carrying three pennies in his pocket—one

Charles Coody, the 1971 Masters champion, is one of many golfers who employ a bit of superstition.

in case one fell out of his pocket, one in case his playing partner didn't have one and needed to borrow Jack's, and one for his own use. Jack also insisted that his former caddie, Angelo Argea, tell him "good luck" on the second hole of a tournament.

- Ben Hogan always preferred using a Titleist No. 4 ball. Sam Snead always had his balls specially made with a "0" for a number. Fred Couples only uses balls marked with an odd number.

- Lee Trevino always wore a red shirt and black pants on the final day of a tournament he had a chance to win. He called it his "payday outfit."

- Jeff Sluman, the 1988 PGA Championship winner, always marks his ball with the head's side face up.

Superstition is usually acquired when a golfer has success doing something a certain way. He'll do anything to recapture the same feeling again, and employing a bit of superstition can sometimes trigger another strong performance.

I've never been a particularly superstitious person. For instance, I don't care what number is on the ball I play, because I go to a new ball several times a round anyway and seeking the same number is just one more thing to worry about. I guess it's just my personal makeup. But if employing a little superstition makes you feel like you have an extra edge, do it.

Diet and Exercise

As I pointed out in the introduction, we have learned a great deal about nutrition and physical conditioning in the last twenty years. The correlation between diet, exercise, and golf is profound. Serious golfers no longer consider the game a peaceful, nontaxing pastime but a test of mental and physical strength and endurance.

The effects of poor conditioning go beyond the physical. When you feel tired and run down, your attitude and your ability

to think clearly changes completely. Feeling weak when your opponent looks strong brings on anxiety, a feeling of ineptitude, frustration, and discouragement.

In the area of nutrition, I realize it is asking a lot of the amateur to alter his diet completely just so he can play better golf. If you are prepared to make a wholesale commitment to changing your diet, fine. There are hundreds of books on the subject, and your doctor can provide helpful advice as well. For our purposes, however, adhering to a few basic principles will make a difference in how you feel and perform. They are fairly easy to follow.

Rule 1: Balance your diet as much as possible. Try to include food from the four basic food groups on a daily basis. That means meat for protein (fish is an excellent substitute if you avoid meat), dairy products such as milk or yogurt for Vitamin D, vegetables, breads and cereals for carbohydrates and fiber, and fruits and vegetables for fiber and Vitamins A and C. The food group neglected most is fruits and vegetables.

Rule 2: Take vitamins. Even if you eat a lot, it doesn't guarantee that you're getting all the vitamins your system requires. Although the value of taking vitamins is questioned in some circles, I have heard far more positive than negative things about taking them. If you tend to eat irregularly, vitamins will help compensate for the lack of vitamins and minerals you derive from solid food.

Rule 3: Cut down on fattening, starchy junk foods. They are high in cholesterol, which is bad for your heart, and sodium, which leads to high blood pressure. Besides, they are just plain fattening.

As a corollary to this, you should moderate your intake of normal sources of fat such as butter, mayonnaise, sour cream, and salad dressings.

Rule 4: Moderate your use of alcohol and tobacco. Golf is played in a social environment where drinking liquor is accepted, even encouraged. A cocktail now and then won't hurt you, but drinking excessively can have a negative effect on your golf.

First, alcohol is fattening. The expression "beer belly" was not created without reason. You can't play your best when you are overweight. Second, alcohol clouds your thinking, not just while you're under the influence but even the day after a party at which you drank heavily. Finally, it not only clouds your thinking but dramatically affects you physically. When you are hung over, you feel weak, shaky, and tired.

If you enjoy drinking, at least moderate your intake the night before a tournament. Make sure you have something in your stomach.

Smoking is a no-no, too. Very few of the young players on the PGA Tour smoke, which is a reflection of the current trend toward discouraging tobacco use. Although there are many cases of good golfers smoking—Bobby Jones, Ben Hogan, Jack Nicklaus, and Arnold Palmer come to mind—cigarettes are definitely bad for your overall health. Some day it might catch up with you.

Rule 5: Don't eat a heavy dinner. You want to eat enough to satisfy both your hunger and your body's food requirements, but eating too much at dinner may prevent you from sleeping well. This, of course, is especially true when you eat late at night. You also may feel sluggish when you wake up the next morning. This rule applies to other meals as well; try to eat small portions of food often rather than gorging yourself at one sitting.

It is worth pointing out, too, that you derive little energy from the food you consumed the night before you play. You get strength and energy from what you ate two and three days before.

Rule 6: Eat a light breakfast. Billy Casper says he plays his best when he feels a little hungry. Ken Green, who won two tourna-

Ken Green is a hearty eater, but he seldom eats any food at all before a competitive round. You probably shouldn't copy Ken, but do avoid eating too much before you play.

ments and more than $750,000 on the PGA Tour in 1988, says he avoids eating anything at all before he tees off. This isn't necessarily recommended for you, but it's worth knowing that when you have lots of food in your stomach, a great deal of blood is sent to your digestive system. This means you will feel drowsy and less alert.

Normally, your body needs two to two-and-a-half hours to initially digest your last meal. Therefore, you not only should eat well before you arrive at the golf course but also eat small portions of easily digested foods, such as an English muffin, a grapefruit, and a bowl of nonsweetened cereal.

Rule 7: Avoid coffee and tea before you tee off. Some golfers like the extra alertness they derive from the caffeine in these drinks, but be careful. Many golfers find that caffeine makes them anxious, fidgety, and nervous. This will cost you on the putting green and can make it difficult to get into a proper rhythm.

Rule 8: Carry high-energy, easily digested snacks in your golf bag. Apples, oranges, trail mix, and raisins are recommended. They are digested quickly for fast energy and, unlike candy bars and other foods containing processed sugar, are synthesized more effectively by your digestive system.

Rule 9: Drink water at regular intervals. This was covered in chapter 2, but it's worth repeating here. Dehydration is dangerous and occurs without your knowing it. Even if you don't feel thirsty, drink water anyway at the rate your body loses it. Don't gorge yourself once or twice a round; doing so may bring on cramps and a bloated feeling. On hot days especially, drink a cup or two of water every hole or so.

Exercise, like diet, is difficult for the golfer to undertake if he is not fit already. I encourage you to do it anyway, however, because the benefits are many. First of all, when you increase your physical strength, you will hit the ball farther with less ef-

fort. You also will improve your touch and feel. Finally, toning and strengthening your muscles increases your endurance, so you will play as well at the end of the round as you did at the beginning.

You need to use care in choosing the types of exercises you do. They should focus on the muscles involved in the golf swing, including the hands, wrists, and forearms; your upper and lower back and stomach; and your legs. The following is a list of fast, easy-to-do exercises for increasing strength, flexibility, and endurance in your golf muscles. I suggest you do them daily.

Caution: Check with your doctor before undergoing any serious exercise regimen.

1. *Swing a weighted club.* Not long after I came to America, I found that if I were to compete favorably on the long courses in this country, I would have to become stronger. Swinging a weighted club did more to increase my distance than any other single exercise. It is particularly useful during the off-season when you can't play regularly. You'll find that by spending fifteen minutes each evening swinging a weighted club, you'll reach your peak much earlier in the season.

Start by swinging the club slowly, at a speed you can control. You want the swing to resemble a real golf swing as closely as possible, and swinging too hard at first will cause your body parts to perform out of sequence. As you feel your muscles loosening, gradually increase the speed and pace of the swings. When you get slightly out of breath, stop. Rest a few minutes and resume. Continue the exercise until you feel a slight burning in your muscles.

2. *Running and cycling.* These also are terrific exercises because they promote all-around muscle conditioning and improve your cardiovascular system. They enhance your ability to control your heart and breathing rate under pressure. How much do you need to do? Not a lot—running a mile or two a day or cycling five miles will quickly bear results.

3. *Walk, don't ride*. I dislike golf carts and prefer to walk when I can. You walk about five miles during a typical round of golf, and the exercise is good at burning calories, strengthening your legs, and conditioning your cardiovascular system. What's more, you'll usually play better when you walk. Walking at an even pace helps you establish a nice inner rhythm. You also are more observant about wind, distances, and the condition of the course.

4. *Trunk rotations*. This stretching exercise is designed to increase flexibility in your torso and lower back. This will help you make a bigger, more controlled backswing turn, leading to more distance.

Place a club across your shoulders and behind your neck with your arms draped over the club. Turn slowly back and through, gradually increasing the length and speed of the turn. Stop when you feel tired. You should eventually work up to forty to fifty turns.

5. *Modified sit-ups*. This is another stretching exercise that increases flexibility in your lower back and the backs of your upper legs. It also strengthens your stomach.

Sit on the floor with your legs outstretched as far as possible. Place your hands under your thighs. Slowly recline until your head touches the floor. Now sit up slowly and try to touch your head on your knees. Repeat ten times; eventually work up to thirty repetitions. Note: It's okay to bend your knees.

6. *Back builder*. The lower back is where most golf-related injuries occur. This exercise strengthens that part of your anatomy. Lay on your stomach with your legs completely outstretched. Clasp your hands behind your neck. Slowly raise your chest and stomach from the floor and, when you can rise no farther, hold that position for five seconds. Repeat. Gradually work up to twenty-five repetitions.

7. *Wrist and forearm strengtheners*. Your hands, wrists, and forearms are the main speed-producing components in the golf

swing. These exercises, requiring five-pound hand weights, will increase your clubhead speed and your ability to control the club through impact.

Sitting down with your back erect, place the hand weights at the base of your fingers with your palms facing up. Let the hand weights pull your hands down so your fingers are pointing almost at the ground. Slowly curl the hand weights toward you, closing your hands as the weights near your forearms. Do ten times nonstop, then repeat.

Now do the same exercise, except this time with your palms facing downward. This will strengthen your wrists and the muscles running along the outside of your lower arms.

8. *Tricep strengthener.* On the downswing, arm speed is mainly obtained through the triceps, the muscles running along the back of your upper arms. This exercise, again using hand weights, will tone and strengthen those muscles.

Hold the hand weight in your left hand and stretch your left arm straight above your head. Grasp your left elbow with your right hand and slowly bend your left arm at the elbow so the hand weight stretches downward behind your back. Do not move your upper arm. When the hand weight descends to shoulder height, slowly elevate the hand weight until your left arm is straight again. Do this ten times, rest, and repeat. Switch the hand weight to your right hand and perform the same exercise.

These are the most effective golf-related exercises I can think of. For a more comprehensive exercise program, send for the book *30 Exercises for Better Golf,* by Dr. Frank Jobe. These exercises are done by many players on the PGA Tour. It is available through the PGA Tour at Sawgrass, Ponte Vedra Beach, FL 32082; phone at 904-285-3700 for cost.

Practice

Although the mental side of golf plays an important role, there is no substitute for building a technically correct, repeating swing. You can have the best attitude in the world, but if your

swing is no good, you will be severely limited in what you can accomplish. There is simply no getting around this fact.

How does practice contribute to the Zone? It inspires confidence, trust, and control under pressure. Knowing your swing leads to a calm, relaxed mental state when the heat is on. You also perform automatically without conscious thought, because practicing grooves your swing so it occurs naturally. Most amateurs view practice as drudgery, but it needn't be that way at all. Ben Hogan is seventy-eight years old and still hits balls almost daily, simply because he enjoys the act of hitting a golf ball. The productivity of your practice, and the amount of enjoyment you derive from it, depends on how you go about it. I was a great practicer early in my career, and I discovered ways to make it pleasant. Here are my keys.

1. *Always practice with a purpose.* If you aren't working on something specific in your swing, you really aren't practicing at all. If you simply get a bag of balls and beat them into the horizon with no purpose, you are as likely to develop bad habits as good ones.

On the other hand, if you have developed a particular problem with your game, such as hitting your pitch shots fat, and devote time, energy, and thought into curing that problem, practice becomes a great deal more interesting. First you search for the problem. In the case of hitting pitch shots fat, it may be that your ball is positioned too far forward in your stance. I find this search challenging and intriguing. Once you identify the problem, you then go about searching for a cure. I always got a lot of enjoyment out of trying new swing techniques until I found one that worked. It is extremely pleasing to come away from the practice tee knowing you've accomplished something positive.

2. *Practice frequently, but keep the sessions short.* One of the great myths about Ben Hogan was that he practiced from sunrise to sunset. Believe me, it wasn't quite that way. I know such practice is impossible, because I tried it at one time.

I found it far more beneficial to practice frequently but to keep the sessions short. There comes a point where practice be-

Ben Hogan winning the 1953 British Open. Today, thirty-seven years later, he still enjoys hitting practice balls.

comes counterproductive. Hitting balls can be tiring, especially if you don't do it every day, and when you tire your muscles don't respond the way they should. You can't tell if a new swing key is working, because you are too tired to perform the key itself.

There is a psychological danger in practicing too long as well. As you tire physically, your concentration span becomes shorter. You are more easily distracted and less alert. Your mind doesn't process the feedback from your body as efficiently. The end result is you get sloppy and realize little benefit from all the time you've put in.

Because of these factors, I recommend you hit no more than fifty balls in a session. Quality, not quantity, is what counts most. Take a brief rest every ten balls or so. Get a drink of water and evaluate your progress. After you've hit fifty balls, stop. You can practice a little later in the day if you like, but space the sessions several hours apart.

3. *Add variation to your practice.* If you are plagued with a duck hook with your driver, don't devote the entire session to improving that one shot. For every three balls where you try to eliminate the duck hook, hit one ball where you try to accomplish something else, like, say, making the ball fly higher than normal. By deviating from your primary purpose once in a while, you get out of the tunnel-vision mode where some parts of your swing are ignored.

I find it useful to work my way through every club in the bag when I practice, ending with the type of shot that is giving me the most trouble. If you are hitting your low irons poorly, for example, start out by hitting a few pitches with your sand wedge, then advance through the other short irons, the long irons, and then your woods. Then go back to your low irons and work on the problem you are experiencing in that area.

4. *Practice with a friend.* Because practicing as often as you should often presents problems with motivation, find a friend who you can encourage and who can encourage you. Make a pact. Agree to practice together three days a week, and don't let

him make excuses for not showing up. Also, tell him not to accept any excuses from you.

When you are on the range together, don't spend too much time socializing. You can, however, arrange contests that will make your practice more interesting. Tour pros sometimes play "call shot," where the player predicts a specific type of shot, such as a high fade, and then tries to bring it off to the satisfaction of his partner. This inspires imagination and creativity. It also makes the game more fun.

5. *Always have a target.* I can't tell you how many times I've asked an amateur in a pro-am where he's aiming on a tee shot and heard in reply, "Somewhere in the fairway." This is obviously an extension of the way he practices. You should always have a specific target. If you don't, you're wasting your time. Simply machine-gunning practice balls accomplishes nothing.

Your target should not just be direction oriented, either. You should pay attention to how far you are hitting the ball as well. That's half the game.

6. *Use alignment aids.* The most common area where pros and amateurs alike go wrong is with alignment. It is extremely easy to fall into the habit of aiming a few yards left or right of the target. When that happens, you are forced to make compensating movements in your swing to get the club moving along the correct target line. Always lay two clubs along your feet when you practice, one positioned just outside the ball pointing at the target, the other placed along your feet, parallel to the first.

7. *Devote half your practice to putting and the short game.* It is ironic to note that, although more than half the shots in golf are played from twenty yards and in, few amateurs devote half their practice to chipping, pitching, and putting. Maybe it's because smashing driver shots to the end of the range is more fun, but in any case it isn't smart. You should practice chipping and putting a lot, because this is where most amateurs perform most poorly.

Seve Ballesteros (to my rear) and me on the practice green: A good portion of your practice should be devoted to putting and the short game.

8. *Practice in all weather and course conditions.* Does the ball fly farther off wet turf or shorter? How does playing bunker shots from wet sand differ from normal sand? What's the best way to keep your grips dry in rainy weather? Do wet greens putt differently than dry greens? Rather than learn the answers to these questions through harsh experience, brave it out and practice under adverse conditions once in a while. You'll be glad you did.

Summary

The techniques discussed in this chapter are the ones I feel are most effective at achieving the Zone and maintaining it. There is more to it than this, of course. The information disseminated in chapters 2, 3, and 4 should be applied in concert with the techniques we discussed here.

As you put these techniques to use, you should frequently evaluate your performance in the areas of what all great players have in common and the elements of the Zone. If you detect a particular weakness, examine the techniques here and determine how you can better apply them.

In chapter 6 we will look into the area of special problems, dilemmas that aren't necessarily improved on by applying the techniques we've discussed so far.

6

Special Problems

Rounding Out Your Mental Approach

When the U.S. Open, the Masters, and a few other important tournaments arrive each year, I take extra measures to prepare my game as thoroughly as possible. I work on my full swing, put in hours on chipping and putting, study the course, and make sure my mental approach is as keen as possible. Nevertheless, I have not always played well in these tournaments.

Looking back, I can see that I was not nearly as prepared as I thought I was. I often overlooked some aspect of the game that didn't seem very important before the tournament arrived. It took some hard experiences to realize that preparing properly means preparing comprehensively for any situation that might arise. You simply can't let any part of the game fall through the cracks when you are getting ready for an important round.

Most golfers tend to work very hard on the noticeable parts of the game, such as the swing, strength and endurance, and the right mental approach. In the meantime, other things drift by the wayside. Your motivation may not be very strong. Maybe you are coming out of a slump. Maybe you are ill-equipped to handle pressure. These are among the problems we'll discuss in this chapter. Learning to devote attention to these areas will round you out as a golfer and competitor.

Staying Motivated

Maintaining peak interest in the game is extremely difficult for amateurs and pros alike. You may love the game deeply and

yearn to excel at it, but sometimes things happen that cause your enthusiasm to wane. It may be a streak of poor playing, where the thrill of shooting good scores is replaced with discouragement and disappointment. Sometimes new and exciting hobbies will temporarily diffuse your interest in golf. Important work and family matters are sure to push golf into the background on occasion.

Fluctuations in enthusiasm are only natural, but the serious golfer pays a price when he stays away from the game for long. Progress made through hard work and application is negated. You can't pick up where you left off; you have to start over. Upon your return you're sure to shoot higher scores, which can be difficult to accept if you are accustomed to playing better. In addition, your peers may have surpassed you, which is always discouraging if you are the least bit competitive.

How, then, can you maintain your zeal for practicing, playing, and competing? I'm especially well qualified to speak in this area, for early in my career I faced a number of setbacks that made me wonder whether I should continue playing golf at all. When I was barely scratching out a living in Australia and on the Asian Tour, it sometimes was extremely difficult to remain committed to the goals I had set for myself. Fortunately, I found ways to stay motivated and interested.

Setting and Meeting Goals

The first thing I learned was how to set goals. Every golfer should strive for a concrete objective, because it intensifies your purpose and provides a reward for your effort. But goal setting can be tricky. You must go about it correctly or else risk doing more harm than good. Follow these rules:

1. *Make your goals realistic.* If you know you will only be able to play or practice twice a week, don't aspire to lower your handicap by ten strokes. If you do you are only setting yourself up for failure and disappointment. Your goals should be challenging yet attainable. At the beginning of the year, honestly assess your time constraints, desire to improve, and natural ability.

2. *Set goals that are game oriented.* Avoid accomplishment-oriented goals such as winning your club championship. If an inconsistent short game is holding you back from competing favorably against the better players at your club, your goal should be more work on chipping and putting. The club championship may come as a result.

3. *Set intermediate goals.* It is easy to lose focus of long-range goals. If you aspire to lower your handicap by five strokes by the end of the year, commit to improving two strokes by May, three strokes by June, and four by July. This will help you monitor your progress and keep you motivated.

4. *Don't be afraid to modify your goals.* If you sense that your ultimate goal is out of sight, don't be discouraged. Set a new one.

Finding Outside Interests

The next thing I learned was that I had to have outside interests. These prevented me from getting burned out. If all you do on weekends is golf, golf, golf, you are certain to grow stale, bored, and, eventually, frustrated.

Bill Rogers, who won the 1981 British Open at Royal St. George's and contended for the 1982 U.S. Open at Pebble Beach, is a self-professed victim of burnout. After he won the British Open, Rogers immediately committed to a heavy tournament schedule overseas, where he played virtually every day without letup. It was a grueling, exhausting grind that took its toll. Within a couple of years, Rogers lost some of his zest for playing and preferred to stay near his home. He still competes on occasion but remains reluctant to rejoin the tour on a full-time basis.

Burnout is very common at the junior level. Many kids are pushed so hard by their parents to play golf all the time that they don't enjoy the good things about being a teenager. By the time they reach their early twenties, they are tired of the game and anxious to catch up on lost time in their personal lives. They

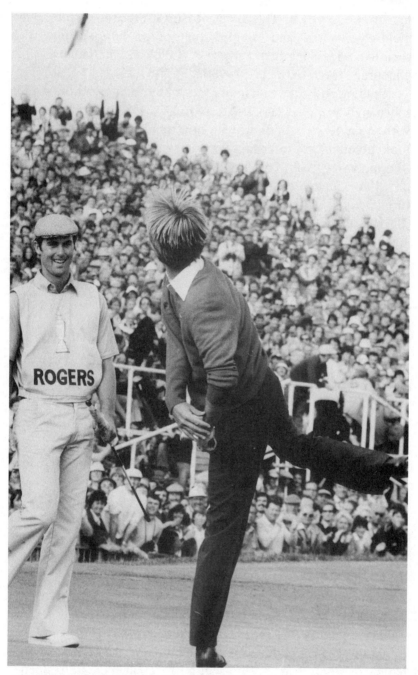

After Bill Rogers won the 1981 British Open, he committed to an exhaustive playing schedule and lost some of his zeal for competition.

hardly ever recover. This is one reason I refuse to dictate to my children, Andrew and Michael, the course they will take with their lives. I will let them make that choice and, in the meantime, encourage them to be well-rounded individuals.

Finding new interests in life was a key to my winning the big tournaments in the late 1970s and early 1980s. Spending time with my wife and children, with my friends hunting and fishing, took me out of my intense, overly serious mode and enabled me to maintain a fresh, enthusiastic outlook on my golf game. Today, I've widened those interests to include golf course architecture and golf club design.

The irony of developing outside interests is that instead of spending less time on your golf game, you'll ultimately spend more because you won't tire of it.

Pride as a Motivator

When the first Legends of Golf senior tournament was announced in 1978, a number of fellows who had retired came out of the woodwork months in advance to get their games in shape. Dr. Cary Middlecoff, Lionel Hebert, Tommy Bolt, and other former stars spent untold hours on the practice range getting ready for this one tournament. Why? Don't think it was the prize money. It was pride. Before these great names would put their games on display, they wanted to make sure they could play well enough to avoid being embarrassed.

One reason Ben Hogan stopped competing when he could still hit the ball about as well as anyone is that he didn't want to play unless he thought he could win. He had too much pride to put anything but his very best game on display. Ben may have gone too far in that regard, but it does show how proud an individual he is and how that pride was responsible for making him such a great player when he was in his prime.

Pride may be the biggest motivator of all, and the only way to obtain it is through accomplishment. If you've lowered your handicap from 10 to 5, you will go to great lengths to keep it there. It isn't much fun to play worse than what you are capable

Tommy Bolt, the 1958 U.S. Open champion, worked hard on his game before returning to compete in the 1978 Legends of Golf tournament. Pride was his chief source of motivation.

of. The reason you took golf seriously to begin with was for enjoyment and the thrill of playing the game well. If you tell yourself that playing well doesn't mean much to you anymore, you're lying to yourself.

Time Management

Because golf has been my full-time calling for almost twenty-five years, I haven't had much problem finding time to play. The amateur is different. With a family and work gobbling up most of his waking hours, the biggest problem sometimes isn't playing well—it's playing, period.

The key here is time management—organizing and prioritizing your activities so you can play more frequently. Leisure time is increasingly difficult to come by these days, and unless you

devote a fair part of it to your golf game, you are lost. You'll progress only so far.

Virtually everyone can manage their time better—at work, home, or on the golf course. It takes thought, discipline, and a sense of organization, but it can be done. In addition to playing a fairly heavy golf schedule these days, I have two young kids, my golf course architecture business, and golf club design responsibilities to worry about. So I've learned a few things about time management.

1. *Determine how important golf is to you.* Before you can set realistic practice and playing goals, you first must decide where golf ranks on your list of other activities. Seek input from your family and be willing to compromise. Evaluate how much time and energy you can devote to the game. When you come to a decision, start looking for ways to maximize your practice and playing time.

2. *Compartmentalize your activities.* Jack Nicklaus has always had the ability to focus solely on the activity he is involved with at a given moment. When he is with his family, he doesn't think about golf. When he is playing golf, he doesn't think about business. That's one reason Jack is so efficient and diverse.

I learned from Jack in this respect. Once, while I was contending in a tournament hundreds of miles from home, my son Michael cut his chin and took six stitches. Maureen didn't tell me about it until the tournament was over, because she knew that (1) the injury wasn't as serious as I might make it out to be and (2) I would be worried and unable to concentrate totally on my game. Another time my home flooded while I was away, and Maureen waited until the tournament was over before telling me.

3. *Make your work and family time more productive.* Obviously, work and family come first. Learn to manage them efficiently so they don't spill over into your golf. Don't waste time at work. Become better organized. Utilize your support staff. At home, concentrate on spending quality time with your wife and

kids. Get off the couch and do things with them. They'll be much happier and more willing to sacrifice on behalf of your golf game.

4. *Think twice before making new commitments.* At the Nabisco Championships at Pebble Beach late in 1988, Greg Norman bemoaned the fact that he was simply doing too much. He was so involved with traveling, performing at corporate outings, making TV commercials, and other activities that he wasn't seeing enough of his family or spending enough time working on his golf game. Greg is such a nice guy that he has a hard time saying no to anyone, but he has since become more discerning in taking on new projects.

When you take on new responsibilities or expand your leisure activities, there's a good chance your golf will suffer. It will be one of the first casualties in your battle to fit everything into your schedule. Think this over before you make new commitments.

5. *Play whenever possible.* Be opportunistic. As a young man, Lee Trevino used to dash out of the golf shop and hit balls in between servicing customers. Ken Green used to sneak onto a private course near his home at dusk just to play a couple of holes before it got dark. They took advantage of every opportunity to play. You can do the same thing. Get up early once in a while and go hit some balls before work. If your wife phones you at work and tells you she's taking the kids shopping and will be late getting home, stop at the golf course and hit a bag or two of balls. Look for openings in your schedule.

The Inevitable Slump

A slump is a temporary decline in performance. A baseball player once likened a slump to a soft bed: easy to get into but hard to get out of. It is one of the most puzzling and distressing phenomena in sport, because no one knows how to prevent a slump or how exactly to get out of one.

Tom Weiskopf described the nature of slumps perfectly.

Slumps are normal and everyone has them. Pros fall into slumps all the time. But whereas pros tend to play their way out of them, amateurs sometimes get so discouraged that they quit playing altogether. This is a groundless reaction, because we now know the causes of slumps and how you can play your way out of them more quickly.

Tom Weiskopf once described the nature of a slump perfectly. "When I'm hitting the ball well, I don't see how I could ever have hit it poorly," he said. "But when I'm in a slump, I don't know how I ever could have hit the ball well."

Slumps in golf have five basic causes.

1. *Making a swing change.* When you alter your technique, your performance often will dip for a while. It takes time for your mind and body to become accustomed to the change. When I played in my first Masters tournament in 1971, I found to my dismay that I hit the ball much too low to play Augusta National the way it ought to be played. Instead of hitting the ball high so it would land softly on Augusta's firm greens, I was stuck with a low, ugly hook. I could barely get a 2-iron shot off the ground. I knew this would be a problem on other American courses as well, and I told Maureen, "Either I am going to learn to play golf properly, or I am going to quit." I was overreacting a bit, but I did need to hit the ball higher if I were to succeed on the PGA Tour.

So, with Bruce Devlin's help, I completely overhauled my swing. I moved closer to the ball at address, weakened my grip, and got a set of irons from Arnold Palmer that were more upright. For two months I practiced like crazy but didn't seem to be making much progress. I was hitting the ball higher but not as consistently as I would have liked. It was discouraging, and for a while I missed more cuts than I made.

Suddenly, everything fell into place. In July I won the Cleveland Open in a play-off with Devlin, the man who helped me make the change. I had my first tour win and, more important, had put an end to the slump.

As you continue to improve your technique, keep in mind

Johnny Miller had a slender build early in his career (left), *but when he bulked up, he fell into a long, discouraging slump.*

that all movements in the golf swing are closely related. If you change one thing, such as your grip, it will demand that you change something else as well. All of the fine-tuning takes time. Be persistent and take heart in the fact that you'll be a better player once you adapt to the change.

2. *Physical changes.* Slumps often result from changes in weight and distribution of muscle mass. Johnny Miller, who in 1974 won eight tournaments and was the tour's leading money winner, once took to doing heavy work around his home. The normally skinny Miller bulked up considerably, adding a lot of muscle to his back, shoulders, and arms. This made it physically impossible for him to swing the club the same as when he was thin. Miller fell into a long slump, going winless for four years. In 1978, he finished 111th on the money list.

Miller's slump was one of the longest on record, and he didn't snap out of it until he adjusted his swing to fit his new physique. His slump ended in 1980 when he won the Inverrary Classic.

Be aware of any changes in your physique. A common reason amateurs start off slowly in the spring is because they put on weight during the winter and find it difficult to make a full turn on the backswing. Their old swing doesn't match their new physique. Only when they lose weight do they start to play better.

Injuries also can lead to a slump, because pain and limited motion in the affected area forces you to make compensating moves in your swing. When the injury heals, you are left with your patchwork swing. If you get hurt, think seriously about laying off for a while. If you must play, however, maintain your same swing but don't swing as hard.

3. *Natural learning plateaus.* Studies on learning show that our application of new knowledge seldom follows a steady, upward pattern. Rather, we tend to reach plateaus where our performance levels off for a while. Such is the case with golf. There will be times when you show no appreciable improvement despite hard work and intelligent thought. This is only natural and you need to persevere through it.

Psychologists aren't sure why these plateaus occur, but it may be that your mind is still processing and adapting to the new information. For instance, when you change your swing from flat to upright, it takes awhile for your body to consistently perform what your mind tells it. Amateurs sometimes mistake this natural process for some error on their part, get frustrated, and return to their old, inferior method. That can be disastrous, for now your mind is trained half one way, half the other. An even longer slump is sure to follow.

4. *Mental changes.* A disruptive life-style, changes in your home environment, and shifting attitudes about your game can also lead to a slump. If your mind is beset by business or family problems, it makes it difficult to concentrate on your game. If a bad round or two brings on a negative attitude about golf, those negative thoughts can snowball and lead to a long, agonizing slump.

Try to stabilize your outlook on golf. Take the bad with the good. If you can maintain an overall positive attitude, you'll be less prone to a slump. And when the occasional slump comes, you'll pull yourself out of it much more quickly.

5. *Increased awareness.* When you learn something new about your swing, there is a tendency to focus on that one element alone. You are inclined to concentrate on how it feels, how it may look, and how it relates to other aspects of your swing. Integrating your new knowledge into your existing skills can be difficult and may lead to a temporary spell of poor play.

The other danger of learning something new is failure to monitor other parts of your swing. Very often, bad swing habits can crop up without your knowing it. As you increase your awareness, don't lose sight of the big picture. Check your entire swing periodically and make sure everything is functioning as it should.

Because the causes of slumps vary, there is no single technique that is guaranteed to pull you out of one right away. I know that taking a few days off seemed to recharge my batteries, and

I approached my slump with a fresh attitude. I also try to recognize that a slump is normal and often a sign of progress.

Perhaps the best advice comes from Harvey Penick, the venerable teaching pro from Texas. He once told one of his star pupils, Ben Crenshaw, "Just remember that it takes just as long to play your way out of a slump as it did to play your way into one."

Preparing for Tournaments

Getting ready for tournament play is as much mental as physical. Ben Hogan once said that casual golf and tournament golf are as different as ice hockey and tennis. The difference is pressure. In tournaments, where it really counts, your emotional state is so different as to truly alter the complexion of the game.

Getting into the Zone is difficult if you are unprepared for the rigors of an important event. If your game is ragged, the techniques described in this book won't suddenly turn it around. Conversely, if your mental approach isn't right, you won't be able to utilize all of your physical skills. The idea is to create a mental climate that is conducive to creating the ideal performance state and to prepare your game so the Zone can bear positive results.

Tournament preparation is a two-stage process. The first stage entails the weeks and days leading up to the tournament. The second stage involves preparing properly the night before, and the day of, the tournament. Here is how to do it.

Early Preparation (Stage 1)

1. *Balance your practice.* Work on all parts of your game and devote particular attention to chipping, putting, and sand play. The reasons are twofold: first, building confidence in your short game will take the pressure off your full swing. Instead of feeling you *must* put the ball in the fairway and *must* hit it on the green, you can relax and let it happen. Second, nervousness tends to have a more debilitating effect on delicate, feel-type shots. If

Ben Hogan playing a practice round prior to the 1953 British Open at Carnoustie, Scotland. Hogan once said that casual golf and tournament golf are as different as ice hockey and tennis.

your chipping and putting are sound, the nervousness won't exact as big a price.

When you practice, visualize the types of shots you will need to hit at the tournament site, and try to copy them. Dave Marr, the 1965 PGA Championship winner, says you should never try to hit a shot in competition that you haven't practiced beforehand. If you create those special shots in practice, you will, in a sense, have experience at hitting them.

As you get your game in shape, avoid making any major swing changes. Go with what you have. Under tournament pressure, a new swing change isn't likely to hold up.

2. *Evaluate the golf course.* Before Ben Hogan played in his only British Open in 1953, he arrived at the tournament site, Carnoustie, weeks in advance. By playing numerous practice

Dave Marr, here winning the 1965 PGA Championship, often says you should never attempt to play a shot in competition that you haven't practiced.

rounds, he discovered where to hit his tee shots so as to create the easiest shot into the greens. He got used to the cold, rainy weather. He perfected the low, run-up-type shots that Carnoustie's firm greens demanded. He became accustomed to Scottish cuisine, found a comfortable place to stay, and got to know his caddie. Predictably enough, Hogan won the tournament.

You can't prepare as thoroughly as Hogan did, but you can learn a lot about the course in advance. Play a practice round or two, if possible. Where are the hazards and out-of-bounds? Are the yardage markers in the fairway accurate? Are the greens and fairways soft or firm?

After you get the answers to these questions, formulate a game plan. Decide which par 5s are reachable in two and which ones require laying up. If a couple of the fairways are particularly narrow, commit to hitting a long iron or fairway wood off the tee. Once you commit to a game plan, remember to stick to it when the tournament comes. Only change it if one of two things happen: (1) the elements intervene, meaning if a par 5 you planned on reaching in two unexpectedly plays into the wind, you may have to lay up or (2) the situation demands that you become more aggressive or conservative. For instance, if someone tells you that a birdie on a difficult finishing hole is necessary for you to finish in first place, you may go for the big drive and daring iron shot.

Next, tailor your practice to fit any unusual shots the course may demand. Don't ignore any part of your game, but spend extra time on areas that may present special problems. If the course has deep rough, practice from the rough. If the sand is especially soft, create some buried lies and practice from them.

If your evaluation of the golf course convinces you to add a specialty club or two to your set, make sure you spend extra time practicing with those clubs. Work on the high, soft "flop shot" you may have to hit with the sixty-degree wedge you've added. Hit some tee shots with the 1-iron you've added for use on some of the narrow par 4s.

3. *Get your house in order.* Organize your work and family activities so you can devote sufficient thought to golf in the days

leading up to the tournament. Avoid arguments and confrontations. If you are filled with worry about nongolf interests before a tournament, it will be more difficult to shift your attention totally to golf.

Get your family involved in your quest. Tell them about the tournament, who's playing in it, some of the history behind it, and why it's important. Delegate some of your responsibilities to them for a little while. The idea is to establish a free, relaxed atmosphere at home and within yourself, so you can give your best effort.

I also recommend you cut your social activities short the last couple of days before a tournament. The things that go with them—late hours, drinking, and so on—can cost you.

Make sure that you take care of as many details as possible. Do you have a ride to the course? Have you found a caddie? Do you need to get your clubs regripped or new spikes put on your shoes? Does the course have a practice area, or will you have to warm up at your home course? Does the course have water available at regular intervals? These are important considerations and should be addressed.

The Night Before and the Day of the Tournament (Stage 2)

1. *Don't alter your routine.* If you always go to bed late, don't try to go to bed early. If you like a nightcap before turning in, have the nightcap. Adhering to your normal habits will lessen your anxiety about the big event.

2. *Do something unrelated to golf.* At this point, you've done about as much as you can to get ready. Dwelling on your performance won't help. Find something to do to get your mind off golf. Play a parlor game with the family, watch television, or read. Your golf-related thinking should not go past double-checking your tee time and choosing the clothes you will wear.

3. *Let your starting time dictate your activity.* Your activity the day of a tournament is extremely important yet often over-looked. Many amateurs simply don't know what to do with themselves. How early should I arrive at the course? Should I practice or just warm up? What should I eat?

I can't answer all of these questions, because a preround reg-imen is highly individual. For instance, some pros like to arrive at the course two hours before their tee time, so they have plenty of time to hit balls and prepare themselves mentally. Others don't like all that time to stew before they tee off and choose to arrive at the course only shortly before they are called to the first tee.

Whatever you decide, it should revolve around your tee time. If you are scheduled to tee off early, get up in time to do everything you normally do, such as read the paper and make breakfast. If you get up even fifteen minutes too late, you'll find yourself rushing around at the last minute. This is bad, because that quick pace may continue during the round. Also, leave yourself an out. If the car doesn't start or you get an emergency phone call, those extra few minutes will come in handy.

If you have a late tee time, get up at your normal hour and go about your business as usual. Avoid doing anything that might make you upset or excited.

How early you arrive at the golf course is important, too. Getting there too early may leave you with a lot to think about but nothing to do. You'll end up turning a four-hour round of golf into an eight-hour round. Show up in time to check in with the officials, inquire about local rules, hit some balls, use the bathroom, and get a drink of water.

4. *Warm up, but don't practice.* The purpose of a preround warm-up is to loosen your muscles and observe what your swing tendencies are that day. Start by stretching slowly. Do some toe touches, trunk turns, and leg stretches. Then make some prac-tice swings with a club, concentrating on smoothness and rhythm. Hit balls with your pitching wedge or 9-iron first, trying only to hit the ball solidly. Progress through the set, hitting just a few balls with each club. You don't want to get tired.

If you don't seem to be hitting the ball very well, don't panic. If your tendency that day is a slight fade instead of a slight draw, review your swing keys and try to detect what's causing the open club face or outside-to-in swing path. If you cannot easily trace the cause, avoid making any drastic alterations in your swing. Go with the slight fade for that day. At least you know where the ball is going. If you try some dramatic correction, such as strengthening your grip twenty degrees, you are headed for disaster.

Pressure and Choking

I hate the word choke. It has terrible overtones. It implies weakness, cowardice, and soft character. It is a label that, ironically, is often placed on someone who has shown a lot of courage just to get into a position where he could fail under pressure.

Although choking is a harsh word that is thrown around much too carelessly, there is such a thing as letting the importance of a situation impair your performance. We all have experienced situations that are so stressful that we are emotionally, psychologically, and physically ill-equipped to handle them. That is when choking occurs. We suddenly lose control—control of our ability to think clearly and perform normally.

Scott Hoch admitted to losing his composure when he three-putted from eight feet on the final hole of the 1987 PGA Championship. He ended up losing by one stroke and said later of the three-putt, "I gassed it."

Seve Ballesteros, firmly in command of the 1986 Masters tournament while playing the final nine holes, suddenly heard several disconcerting crowd roars as Jack Nicklaus reeled off a string of birdies to get back in contention. Obviously rattled, Seve dumped a simple (for him) 4-iron approach shot into the water at the fifteenth hole.

Doug Sanders, facing a three-foot putt to defeat Jack Nicklaus on the last hole of the 1970 British Open, spasmodically pushed the ball wide of the hole. He lost the play-off the next day.

When Doug Sanders missed this putt that would have won the 1970 British Open, some observers claimed he choked. In truth, Sanders merely had difficulty adapting to the nature of the situation.

These are a few examples of what some people would call choking. But instead of defining the phenomenon as some chickenhearted reaction to pressure, I prefer the definition offered by 1964 U.S. Open champion Ken Venturi. "Choking is only unfamiliarity with the situation," says Venturi. "After you have been in a certain situation a few times, you learn how to handle it."

I totally believe that. Pressure is relative. A tour pro who has a five-foot putt to win is under no more pressure than the amateur who faces a five-footer to win the club championship. The amateur, you see, is out of his element. Although the outcome may not be as important, his lack of familiarity with the situation makes him feel pressure just as dramatically as the pro.

I also think pressure is overrated. From a distance of eight feet, the best players in the world will make about 50 percent of their putts. But when they miss the eight-footer under pressure, people are quick to say that they choked. In fact, they may have had nerves of steel but simply fell victim to the percentages.

Still, pressure and choking can be very real. When pressure becomes overwhelming, a number of things happen physically. Your chest tightens and you have difficulty swallowing, which is where the expression choking probably originated. Your heart pumps faster, your hands start shaking, your knees quiver, you become nauseated, start sweating, and your vision jumps and blurs. Your body is quite literally unable to function normally.

The physical reactions are merely a response to a wild emotional state. You feel afraid, panicky, awkward, and nervous. Your thoughts race out of control. Self-confidence is replaced with self-consciousness.

I have felt these sensations. I have choked, too. However, my experiences came early in my career and I've been fortunate enough not to throw a PGA Tour event away because I was out of control. I've learned to combat pressure and you can, too.

Because choking begins in the mind, the best way to prevent it is to change your perception of pressure situations. Try these tricks.

1. *Concentrate on execution, not the outcome.* Kathy Whitworth, one of the great woman golfers of all time, once missed

Kathy Whitworth, one of the great woman players of all time, once learned a valuable lesson about thinking constructively.

a four-foot putt that would have tied her for first place in an LPGA tournament. In the press room afterward, Whitworth said, "I was thinking about how badly I needed to make the putt instead of what I had to do to make the putt."

When you start thinking about the importance of a particular shot, you are in serious trouble. Such thoughts breed anxiety, nervousness, and fear. They will snap you right out of the Zone. Instead, you should focus solely on execution, the swing keys that will help you bring off a good shot.

Apply the techniques in chapters 3, 4, and 5. Concentrate on your preshot routine, on staying in rhythm. Keep your muscle tension level low, your thought process calm.

2. *Change your attitude about mistakes.* Early in my career I was a painstakingly slow player who studied every shot so intensely as to drive my playing partners crazy. I felt I had to do this to avoid making mistakes. I told myself mistakes could not be tolerated, especially under pressure. I believed that errors reflected some kind of inner weakness. With that kind of thinking, I probably made just as many mistakes and compounded them by reacting viciously against myself.

One day I realized and accepted that everyone makes mistakes and the best way to prevent them was through sound technique, thorough preparation, and simple concentration. I directed my energy to the real causes of mistakes and began making fewer of them. And when I did make a mistake under pressure, I tried not to let it affect me as much.

3. *Tell yourself, "I deserve to be here."* It's strange, but golfers will work like hell to attain a certain playing goal and then, when they are on the brink of achieving it, ask themselves, "Do I deserve to be here? Am I worthy of the accomplishment? Do I belong on the list of other players who have won this tournament?"

This is choking in its most subtle form. It usually occurs when you are on the verge of accomplishing something greater than you ever have before. Thoughts that never entered your mind before suddenly run rampant. "What about the tournament

next week? People will expect me to win that one, too." Or, "I've hit so many bad shots. Will people think I'm a fluke?"

Tell yourself you deserve it! You've earned the right to be in this situation. It's what you've dreamed of, what you've worked for months to achieve. Be a little selfish. This is the moment you've been waiting for, so bring it home in style.

4. *Whether you win or lose, it won't change your life.* Sure, winning matters. That's why they keep score. But you have to keep competition in perspective. If you win, your wife will still love you and your friends will still like you. If you lose, those facts won't change. Your performance is not a total reflection of you as a human being. Sports is but one part of life, a piece of a greater whole.

5. *Alter your perception about pressure.* Pressure is something you put on yourself. If you perceive a situation as filled with pressure, that's what you'll feel. On the other hand, if you look at it as an opportunity to have fun and perform your best, the situation will take on a different complexion. Important? Yes. Serious? Sure. But life threatening? Of course not. If you feel threatened in competition, you will respond in a threatened way.

To a great extent, you can't talk yourself into believing that what you're doing has no importance. Your hard work, love of the game, and zest for competition speaks to the contrary. Nevertheless, don't lose sight of the fundamental reason for playing to begin with: fun.

6. *Focus on what TO do instead of what NOT to do.* When a competitor feels the first effects of pressure, his first instinct is to try to control the emotional and physical reactions to it. Such thoughts as, "don't shake," "don't be nervous," and "don't hurry" pervade your mind. This is the wrong approach. For one thing, focusing on those reactions to pressure usually exacerbates them. Second, you channel your thinking away from the positive things you can be doing to divert pressure.

Think of what TO do. Focus on positive thoughts and tech-

niques that will enable you to perform well. Tell yourself, "take a deep breath," "this is fun, I can't believe how excited I am," "keep your muscles loose." These thoughts will counteract your response to pressure and help you assert yourself.

Although these keys are a big help, the best way to learn to handle pressure is to be under pressure as often as possible. Play in more tournaments. Step up the amount of your bets on weekends. Set higher goals. People respond to pressure differently, and the only way to ascertain how you respond to it is to experience it.

7

Monitoring Your Mental Toughness

Some Final Tips on Keeping the Zone Intact

Professional golfers know the Zone to be a fragile, elusive mental state that is often difficult to obtain and even harder to preserve on a consistent basis. For amateurs, the challenge is even greater. Although athletes and sports psychologists have discovered many techniques to help all golfers achieve the ideal performance state (and they are investigating even more), in many ways the Zone remains a rather puzzling phenomenon.

The information I've disseminated to this point is valid and is as practical as I could make it. Yet it also is extensive. Because the Zone requires delicate balancing of so many components, I suspect that some of you may at some point become discouraged by your inability to get into the Zone as frequently as you would like.

That discouragement is unnecessary and is the reason this final chapter is necessary. Poor execution of the Zone is due, in almost every instance, to improper utilization of one small but critical skill area. Inadequate performance in that one area often has a carryover effect into other skill areas, giving you the illusion that the whole system has disintegrated.

Identifying those skill areas, increasing your awareness of them, monitoring them, and then addressing them effectively is the key to obtaining the ideal performance state on a consistent

basis. Here are those problem areas and some solutions to strengthening them.

Self-Confidence

Carryover effect: influences calmness, physical relaxation, anxiety level, visualization skills, ability to control thoughts and emotions.

Self-confidence is knowing you can perform well. As I explained in chapters 3 and 4, self-confidence is a trademark of every good golfer and is a vital element of the Zone. Regardless of your level of physical talent, weak self-confidence will seriously curtail your performance.

Maintenance strategies:

1. *Increase your physical strength and endurance.* Improving your diet, becoming more fit, and practicing more frequently will elevate your self-image and ability to think positively.

2. *Set realistic goals.* Nothing boosts your confidence like achievement. Establish some reachable practice and playing goals and work hard to attain them. Your sense of self-worth is sure to increase.

3. *Increase self-discipline.* My years of hard, disciplined practice imbued me with the satisfying knowledge that I was in total control of myself. Establishing a pattern of self-reliance increases your trust and inner strength.

4. *Use positive visualization.* Review the section on visualization set forth in chapter 5. Make sure you create only positive mental pictures at home and on the golf course.

Concentration (Attentional Control)

Carryover effect: influences anxiety level, effortless performance, automatic reactions, alertness.

Concentration is measured by how well you eliminate

distractions, feelings of self-consciousness, and unimportant thoughts. Absorbing yourself in your golf game and excluding all superfluous thoughts and emotions will prevent a host of related problems.

Maintenance strategies:

1. *Work on staying calm and quiet inside.* In between shots, take Sam Snead's advice and think "cool" thoughts. Getting too excited, thinking about the consequences of a shot, or getting angry at yourself over a mistake will disrupt your ability to focus on your game.

2. *Stay in the here and now.* Golf is played one shot, one hole, at a time. Avoid dwelling on past and future events during your round.

3. *Practice concentrating.* PGA Tour commissioner Deane Beman, a fine touring pro during the 1960s, is one golfer who believes it is possible to practice concentrating. During long plane flights, Deane says he would focus his eyes on a spot on the cabin wall and see how long he could keep them there. Beman always had excellent powers of concentration, and this was one way he kept himself sharp.

A more practical way to practice concentrating is to do it during practice. As you hit each ball, keep your mind focused on your preshot routine, inner rhythm, and your mental imagery. Don't let anything distract you. Monitor how often your concentration was broken by an outside event or how frequently your mind wandered onto something unrelated to golf.

Poor Control of Negative Energy

Carryover effect: influences mental calmness, physical relaxation, anxiety level, optimism, enjoyment, alertness, self-confidence.

Failing to control negative emotions such as fear, anger, frustration, envy, and resentment is a chief reason many golfers

"beat themselves" in competition. When things aren't going well for you, this is one of the first areas you should check.

Maintenance strategies:

1. *Increase your awareness.* Monitor your physical, mental, and emotional responses to pressure. You're likely to find that you don't react the same way every time. Get to know yourself and the situations that cause fear, anger, and frustration so you can deal with them accordingly.

2. *Control your thinking.* When Kenny Knox won his first PGA Tour event, the 1986 Honda Classic, he faced an incredibly difficult bunker shot on one of the final holes in the last round. A negative mind-set would have made a good shot impossible. Knox said but one thing to himself: "Make the shot. Just make it." Sure enough, he holed the shot and then hung on to win.

If, like Knox, you can control your thoughts and feelings under pressure, you'll succeed more often than you'll fail. Knox understood at that critical moment that his ability to play the shot well depended on how strictly he could control his thinking.

3. *Enhance your visualization skills.* When your emotions are playing havoc with you under pressure, you can eliminate negative thoughts by picturing pleasant, tranquil scenes. I've done this many times. Instead of focusing sharply on immediate, pressure-inducing thoughts, learn to relax by letting your mind drift to relaxing scenes and images. There's no better way to lessen tension.

4. *Play in the here and now.* A sure sign of poor concentration is thinking ahead to what holes you or your opponent will receive a handicap stroke on, what's going on in other matches, and how well you need to play the rest of the match in order to win. I can't say it enough: the only thing that matters is what's happening now. Learn to focus on the moment.

5. *Start feeling good about you.* Your perception of yourself off the golf course can have an immediate effect on how well you

perform on the course. Improve your dress and physical appearance. Improve your performance at work and your relationships with other people. If you like yourself, you'll improve your self-confidence, energy, attitude, and desire.

Visualization and Imagery Skills

Carryover effect: influences calmness, enjoyment, effortless performance, automatic responses, self-control.

Jack Nicklaus has talked about "going to the movies" or seeing in his mind's eye the shot or swing he was about to execute. Because your central nervous system can't differentiate between vivid mental pictures and an actual physical event, learning to visualize sound swing mechanics and a desired ball flight will often make it happen.

Although visualization usually refers to physical performance, you can also benefit by imagining how you will react to certain pressure situations. When golfers talk about having a five-foot putt in practice to "win the U.S. Open," they are mainly trying to create the right emotional climate.

Maintenance strategies:

1. *Practice sharpening all of your senses.* Every one of your five senses plays a role in golf, even your senses of smell and taste. A dry mouth, for example, can tip you off that you're feeling a little pressure. The next time you practice, devote one sense to each shot you hit. On one shot, concentrate only on what you see. On the next ball you hit, think only of your sense of touch. Do the same with hearing, smell, and taste. Become familiar with all of your senses, and you'll have a more comprehensive command over your thinking and physical actions.

2. *Use photographs, mirrors, or film.* Some golfers learn faster by watching themselves and others perform. You may find it useful to view a videotape of yourself or a top pro swinging and then transfer a specific action to your own swing. This is especially true when you are playing well. Have someone take some pictures of your swing, and, when you fall into a slump, study

the photos and try to recapture the same mechanics. Visualizing a good swing will help you imitate it.

3. *Rehearse your performance in advance.* If you fear that an upcoming tournament may be jarring and difficult to deal with, mentally walk through the experience beforehand. Sit in a soft chair and imagine yourself arriving at the tournament site, parking the car, going to the locker room, checking in at the official table, fetching some practice balls, meeting your playing partners, and teeing off. Take your time and concentrate on detail. If you do this carefully, you'll find you'll already have "played" in the tournament before you tee off. It's a great way to decrease tension and fear.

Self-Motivation

Carryover effect: influences physical relaxation, emotional energy, optimism, enjoyment, effortless performance, alertness, self-control.

Many amateurs (and a lot of pros) suspect that motivation is something you either feel or you don't. That simply isn't true. Feeling eager to play and compete is a skill that can be enhanced by using several techniques. It is important that you learn them, because every golfer will go through periods where practice seems like drudgery and the rewards of competing simply don't seem to be worth the price you pay in time and effort.

Maintenance strategies:

1. *Review your goals and establish new ones.* Practicing, watching your diet, and studying the golf swing are pleasurable pursuits, but they can be overdone. When your enthusiasm for these constructive acts wanes, you need to remind yourself why you are doing them. Examine your goals and your progress toward them. If they seem a little farfetched, set new ones that are challenging yet obtainable. Also set intermediate goals to help keep your long-term objectives in sight.

2. *Keep reminders of your successes present.* I don't feel it's too egotistical to hang a photo of my winning the 1981 U.S. Open on the wall of my den. It reminds me why I've practiced so hard and how that practice proved worthwhile. Keep a scrapbook, hold on to scorecards of your best rounds, think back to a nice compliment you may have received from a better player than yourself.

3. *Seek out support.* Let your family and closest friends in on your ambitions in golf. They can be a great source of encouragement.

4. *Make the game fun again.* During a practice round at the Colonial National Invitation last year, Mac O'Grady, Ted Schulz, David Ogrin, and Kenny Knox played a match with an inventive format: they hit their tee shots and putts at the same time. This provided a lot of laughs and at the same time gave them a preview of the golf course. If the game starts to get tiresome, inject some imagination into your practice and casual rounds. It's a great way to remind yourself that golf, for all its trials, is still a game.

5. *Associate with highly self-motivated golfers.* Enthusiasm and a strong work ethic are contagious. Playing with fellows who take the game seriously and strive to improve at it will encourage you to do the same.

Mental Toughness Training for Golf